What readers have said about *Before You Go*

D1136739

Before You Go

The ultimate guide to planning your gapyear

third edition

Did you want me to go?
I didn't know,
But I went.
You didn't stop me,
Were you proud?
I came back,
To your relief.
I had changed,
For the better,
...my life had begun.

Dedicated to:
Mum and dad who have eventually become resigned to my itchy feet, brothers Mat and Rob for always being older and fatter than me (which will be a blessing in the years to come), Claire for her amazing support and encouragement in making this book a reality, the lovely Anne James and Michael Palin for taking an interest... and of course Tony, who accompanied my first steps, and from where it all began.

There are now a few other people in my life who deserve a mention. Peter, the left arm to my right, for accompanying me to hell and back on this crazy gapyear mission; Carolyn for always being there, laughing and smiling throughout no matter what; and now Jack, my first nephew... for being the coolest little one-year-old in the world!

Tom's Disclaimer
I have written this book with the view that you are not muppets, but intelligent young people. Therefore I expect everything I talk about to be taken with a pinch of salt, and any decisions you take to be of your own free will. If you choose to run off a cliff, under a bus, or marry a nun – it's not my fault, and so I take no responsibility for your actions. Act on my advice as you wish, but you can't blame me for your actions.

Although I make every effort to ensure the accuracy of all of the information in this book, changes occur incessantly. I cannot therefore take responsibility for facts, addresses and circumstances in general that are constantly subject to alteration.

Now... get on with reading the book!

'A journey of a thousand miles must begin with a single step.'
Lao Tzu, Chinese philosopher.

You've just taken it.

Before You Go

The ultimate guide to planning your gapyear

third edition

Tom Griffiths

foreword by
Michael Palin

BLOOMSBURY

A BLOOMSBURY REFERENCE BOOK

Third edition published in Great Britain 2003
Second edition published 2002
First published in 1997. Reprinted 1999

Bloomsbury Publishing Plc
38 Soho Square
London W1D 3HB

British Library Cataloguing-in-Publication Data
A catalogue record for this book is available from the British Library

ISBN 0 7475 6638 0

Design and production by Navigator Guides
Printed and bound in Italy by Legoprint

Every effort has been made to ensure that the information in this guide is
accurate and up to date and the advice is given in good faith. However, neither
the publisher nor the author is responsible for any problems encountered
before or during your travels.

Contents

About the author

June 21st 1974 I arrived on the scene in Ipswich, Suffolk. Grew up in a little village called Stratford St Mary on the Suffolk side of the Essex/Suffolk border. Spent 10 happy years at Ipswich School where my writing skills were 'honed' by the likes of Messrs Goodhand and Prior...

After completing A-levels I took a gapyear and went travelling round the world with my long-time school-friend Tony. This was our first big trip - probably similar to any that a reader of this book may be about to do. We plodded off out via America, Hawaii, Fiji, then had a fantastic few months in Australia. For the return leg we hopped back over Indonesia, Singapore, Malaysia and Thailand before returning back to Blighty. The following summer I took a trip to North America which saw me hitch-hike solo over 5,000 miles across Canada, then travel down into America, visiting friends at universities and others working on the infamous 'kids camps'. South America, the African continent and trips to the Poles were next on the list.

After that I went to Manchester University, graduating with a 2:1 in Economics. I busked on the street with my didgeridoos for cash and a bit of a laugh, and raised money for the Essex Voluntary Association for the Blind, for whom I ran the London Marathon. At the time of writing the first edition of this book I was 22 years old, and still buzzing from four years of amazing experiences.

Since then I have won the 'Young Travel Writer of the Year Award' and set up The Gapyear Company with co-founder Peter 'oim a Cornish bumpkin' Pedrick. The two of us now run the largest gapyear community in the UK with www.gapyear.com, gapyearmagazine, www.gapyearshop.com, www.insureyourgap.com, www.travelhealthcentre.com and a whole host of other random gapyear stuff. I am also the media spokesperson for the gapyear industry, appearing regularly on television, radio and in the print media commenting on gapyears and youth travel. Still awaiting a knighthood and a named bench outside the Post Office in Stratford St Mary...

So in a brief nutshell, that's me! I'm just the average sort of guy about town, with loads of dreams and ambitions just like everyone else... and if you see me, why not buy me a pint?

Photo by Basil Pao

Foreword

By Michael Palin

I was once taken to task for being obsessed with toilets and bowel movements in my television documentaries. I make no apologies for being a toilets before temple traveller. Too often, travel is presented as a series of glamorous getaway moments, glorious sunsets, colourful markets, elegant buildings and sublime contemplations of the beauties of creation.

These may well be the sort of things that make us want to set out in the first place, but such pleasures are subjective. One traveller can find sublime happiness on a Polish cargo boat, another on the rim of a volcano, another in a Mayan temple.

What the departing traveller needs to know is not so much other people's opinions of what's wonderful, but basic, unromantic, mundane and absolutely essential advice on how to get to these wonderful things and what to do when you get there and find you have diarrhoea, sunburn and no money to get back. This is why I think Tom Griffiths's book is useful and valuable and quite possibly indispensable. It is a treasure-trove of helpful information for young travellers (and old ones too). It's clear, comprehensive and written with wisdom and humour. It has answers to just about every question you could and should ask before setting out. He even has a section called Coming Home – the first time I've seen this interesting phenomenon dealt with in any travel guide. It is a real problem as I discovered on my return from going Around the World in Eighty Days. I found myself shunned at parties – after all, what do you say to someone who's just been round the world? If you have the urge to travel you should read this book – before, during and after you go – AND it makes wonderful toilet paper.

www.fco.gov.uk/knowbeforeyougo

Taking a gapyear is a great opportunity for young people to broaden their horizons, making them more mature and responsible citizens. Our society benefits from travel, which promotes character, confidence, decision-making skills and an awareness of other people and cultures. But we need to ensure that the gapyear experience is not spoilt by unnecessary problems or accidents. Time spent in advance on research and preparation can save a great deal of trouble and heartache later.

We are delighted to be working in partnership with gapyear.com on the 'Know Before You Go' campaign. It is essential that all first-time travellers prepare before they travel – that they have proper insurance cover, they have read the FCO Travel Advice for where they're going, and they know how we can, and cannot, help them if they get into trouble. I encourage all travellers to check out our website at www.fco.gov.uk/knowbeforeyougo before travelling overseas.

The Rt Hon. Jack Straw MP
Secretary of State for the Foreign Office

Author's preface

‘ *Travel teaches toleration* ’ **Henry Ford**

Every once in a while journalism portrays backpacking to be dangerous, and then in the same breath reports that Elvis is alive and running a chippy in Peckham. Make of it what you will!

So what is this book about?

Hi there!

This book has been written for one purpose and one purpose only – to get you started. Travelling is one of the most awesome things you can do in your life and has definitely been the best thing that has ever happened in my life, next to the trials and tribulations of my football team of course – Ipswich Town. I have had some wicked moments all over the world and have noticed the positive influence it has had on my life. It has been such an awesome thing in my life that I now aim to make it my life's ambition to spread the word and attempt to make as many people think about doing a bit of travel in their life.

Unfortunately many people want to travel but the majority bottle out. Why? Well, for all sorts of reasons, everything from not having the money to not wanting to leave the love of their life. Most just see all the hassly bits of sorting out flights, visas, money, relationships, work, uni, etc., etc., and can't be bothered! Hopefully, this is where I come in.

I have 'been there, done that'. Most importantly I have recently been in the position that you are in now... you're apprehensive, daunted by the whole thought of actually going away to distant places, and possibly confused as to how to approach it all, i.e. what tickets to buy, backpack to take, insurance to get, etc., etc., etc.

Yet on the other hand you are, deep down, excited about the prospect of taking time out to 'discover the world', and in doing so discover more about yourself. The more you hear stories from people who have 'been there, done that', the more you want to go... suddenly they're not travel bores any more, but 'gurus' who give you visions of tropical islands and fun in the sun! Well, it's all out there waiting for you, you've just got to go for it!

A great authority on the subject of travel?... not me, I'm just 'Tom'!

I am no Shakespeare. I am not actually a writer, as you are about to see! Having spent my youth on the sportsfields rather than with my head in books, I would always get bored whenever I picked up a book. I therefore thought that if I could write a book that I would read, then anyone could read it. This book is therefore very real, as I don't pull punches and don't expect to spoonfeed you all the way. Hopefully, I will enable you to think for yourself on a subject you may not know a lot about at the moment and as a result point you in the right direction... all the way to the airport.

What will you get from this book?

This book will get you started. It has worked for others and I hope it will work for you. It is not flash, it is not rocket science, it is just simple. I have enlisted the help of a few people here and there: Tony – my first travelling partner; Tim – a school-friend; Colin – a uni mate; cousin Helen; and various others. They are mentioned on the odd occasion to add relevance to a point. Unfortunately for them, 'names have not been changed to protect the innocent', and so humiliation may be the outcome. We have all been in your position, all not really known what to do, and have asked advice from others... advice we have followed, practically to the letter. Most of it has been really useful, and the rest, well, as you can imagine... your Grandad telling you how to avoid sharks in the southern hemisphere (like he did during the war!)... really won't get you very far, fascinating though it is!

We want to help you, as we ourselves have been helped. You can take our advice or leave it, but it will get you started before you go, give you ideas, make you think, and help you come up with some decisions.

There is so much pathetic advice out there which is about as useful as Bernard Manning's 'Top Tips For Firm Buttocks'. People are even trying to give it to me to put in to this book... 'Don't forget to warn people that if they walk the streets of Sydney at night that they have a 1 in 3 chance of being attacked.' I mean... come on, give me a break!

> ➤ You will not find this book jam-packed with my 1,001 great travelling stories (to the great relief of my friends!).

> ➤ It is not a book telling you what to do and where to go in all the countries you may like to visit.

For these, simply look at the shelves bursting at the seams around you! Novels such as *On the Road* by Jack Kerouac, and the various Michael Palin books, are perfect for whetting your appetite for travel stories and travel (look in the back under '**Good books on the market**'). The Lonely Planet, Rough Guide and Footprint books are all fantastic as guides for the countries in which you wish to roam.

A quick point about reading the book...

Because there is so much that applies to everyone from 'across all the borders', I do advise you to read the book from cover to cover, and not skip out the bits about male travelling just because you are female, or vice versa. So much applies to both sexes that **I have written the book in such a way that it is important to read it all the way through**. If I had made it specific in parts, it would have ended up as a long list of boring facts, figures and thoughts. I have therefore decided to bring up points in the various sections to put it all in context and to try and make it more readable. Are you as confused about what I am trying to say as I am? OK, a few examples needed.

- In the chapter **Parents** I bring up the issue of 'keeping in touch' whilst travelling. A few ideas, tips, etc., one of which is 'Post Restante'. Intrigued by this? Then go and read about it...
- In the chapter **Male solo** I talk about a few personal experiences, 'culture shock', meeting people, travelling around, etc.
- And in **Female solo**, I address issues such as awareness of other cultures, work, etc.

In the three points highlighted above there is something there for everyone, and they're written as part of a text that won't/shouldn't send you to sleep. So to do justice to the book, please read all the way through... it's not very long, and if I can do it, then you certainly have no excuse!

If you are aged 17–24 then you are at the perfect age to travel

At the moment you have no real commitments. You may think you do, but unless you have a house, mortgage, two children, a spouse, car, job, debts, and a dog called Gerald, you are not a fully fledged member of the 'rat race', and you won't be for another few years yet. However, once you get your membership card and enter it, then commitments make travel like this virtually impossible. You've got to do it now!

The same old routine... break from it!

There is a lot of pressure to follow routine, i.e. GCSE's, 'A' levels, university, job or any variation around that... maybe starting work just after GCSEs or 'A' levels. There is a worry about taking time out and wasting time, but...

➤ What is the difference between working 43 years instead of 44?

Taking time out before university?

Lots of people do it, plus it gives you a well-earned break between four years of working for exams, and another three (minimum).

Remember that it is encouraged by universities, as you are seen be be more mature and so ready for the challenges of higher education. Anecdotally, fewer people drop out after year one who took a gapyear than those who didn't.

It is also seen by others as the break between being a teenager and an adult.

The same applies for after university/college

You are graduated, qualified... what for?

- not too sure about what direction you want to go in (like me, right at this minute)?
- need something to fill in all those blank bits on the CV and on the application forms?
- want to become more employable?
- or do you just need a break?

THEN GO!

I've harked on long enough... there's a world out there... go and see it, and live life to the full! So... if you need some friendly advice to help to kick the ball and start it rolling *before you go*

...THEN READ ON

Chapter 1

So why travel?

'*If you think you can, you can;
and if you think you can't,
you're right* **Henry Ford**

Follow your dreams

Have you got an answer to the question: Why travel?

'I suppose I should do because everyone else is doing it.' *Wrong answer, think again*! Everyone else seems to be buying Playstations and putting dodgy tunes on their mobiles, but that doesn't mean that you're going to catch me doing it.

Maybe you just want to impress your friends?

Yet again, I think that you're barking up the wrong tree here. How impressed will they be, if you have a bad time and end up coming back early? Hardly going to be queuing up to buy you a pint now are they! *Think again*!

Going travelling could be an easy excuse for you to get out of something

Running away from a girl/boyfriend/the law/parents/psychotic grannies, other pressures on you like debt or exams, or maybe you just don't want to be somewhere for the time being. Need I say it... wrong! It's not all going to go away just because you have for a while.

Factors like boredom, lack of opportunity or dead ends wherever you look may well spur you on to travel, but at the end of the day it must be because you want to travel. **You** want to see the world. **You** want to see life. **You** want to appreciate life. Maybe you can use it as an opportunity to 'find yourself'.

➤ Your decision, your life. So do it for yourself and for no one else.

The time is right

Every year, more and more people of our age are going off travelling around the world... hundreds of thousands a year. If you think about it, you probably know of someone who is doing it at the moment. Therefore if most people know of someone doing it, then can you imagine the number of backpackers out there? It is easy for me to say it and imagine it as I've 'been there, done that', but unless you have seen towns virtually full of backpackers, you can easily be led to believe that you are going to be on your own out there. **This is simply not the case**, and it's something that I'm going to try and ram home over the course of this book.

- With the increase in demand, prices for flights and travel in general are coming down the whole time, so **it's never been cheaper to travel**.
- As a result of this massive increase in demand, **it's also never been easier to travel**, with youth travel companies popping up all over the place, as well as tour operators, coach routes, discount accommodation, Internet cafes, advice centres blah blah blah blah blah....

Let's take Australia for example

The number one destination for backpackers. The day you land in Sydney, so will hundreds of others... all about to do the same as you. Buses go up and down the coast from Sydney to Cairns every day. You don't have to lift a finger it's so easy. Get on a bus, and at the next town get off... to be met by representatives from the various hostels with free mini buses. Having spoken to a few people in Sydney you'll already know which one you want to go to, and so you jump on their bus. When you decide to move on, they take you back to catch the bus, you go to the next town... where it is exactly the same. It's actually too easy!

However, it's not just Australia, as all over the world there is a well-trodden backpacker trail. Everyone you meet will be on it or will have been on it. Every time you meet up with someone you'll swap a few ideas over a beer or two, and you'll soon know where you should be heading, and what to do when you get there. If you find it too easy, you can make it more difficult for yourself – if not, don't bother! So what are you worried about? 'Well now you've mentioned it, Tom, nothing... but no one's told us this before.' Well, it's about time that they did... so now I have. I do appreciate that until you have tried it you're going to be a bit sceptical, so I'm afraid all I can do on this one is say 'trust me!'

What are you going to come up against?

What do you come up against in life anyway? Highs and lows of course. So why should this be any different? These are some reasons:

- challenges
- the odd bit of danger and excitement
- poverty may run up behind you and smack you in the face...
  that'll make you think a bit, it did me!
- you'll have to live out of your backpack
- looking after yourself when you are ill
- facing up to every problem and decision that you are going to meet.

On the other hand you'll learn:

- independence
- self-reliance
- and the appreciation of people and the things around you.

You are going to learn more about the world and realise that there is more to life than your local night-club and the odd snog at ten-to-two.

Does what I have just said give you a nervous, but exciting buzz? If so, then you are definitely going to have a lot of fun!

Furthermore, when you come back, you'll be able to answer those questions on TV quiz shows and 'Trivial Pursuit' that leave most people looking as blank as a baffled trout... **so which south-east Asian island does the Equator run through?**

You'll know damn well that it is Sumatra, as you spent four hellish days in the back of a bus trekking up to the bloody thing, squashed in between 10 chickens and a goat, the latter of which gave birth, giving you a too close for comfort experience that made you glad you'd nicked the sick bag off the plane!

Therefore when it came to that question in 'Trivial Pursuit', you shout out the answer with glee, and when about to expand on your experience you get cut down by your mate saying 'Oh guess what, I bet Tom's bloody been there an' all', so you pick up the next card and play on. And that's what they call... life!

Getting back to the working habit

Admittedly it does take a bit of adjusting, but you'll soon get back into it all. The main problem is this great habit whilst travelling of getting up when you like/when the mood takes you. If at this point you decide that you want to stay wherever you are – you stay. If not – you go! It's as simple as that. If you are a naturally free-spirited person, then your spirit literally does go free, leaving you happy to wander, explore, discover and learn.

When you get back to the UK, you will probably find that everything seems to be moving a lot quicker than your own relaxed way of life, so quick that you often feel 'spaced' and dizzy for a couple of days when you return. This all depends of course where your last 'port of call' was, whether the urban rush of Los Angeles, or the tropical haven of Thailand. And then you are required, by other people, to be in the office for 9am, have an hour for lunch, and then to finish at 5pm. Or you may be a student, and have to be in a lecture theatre for 10am, have a tutorial at 11am, and have to follow deadlines and time schedules. But then we all know that taking it in your stride and at your own pace is the beauty of university. You can either be an eager busy little bee (like I was at university!), or you can be like a certain housemate of mine who, during three years of university, only went to the library once... and that was only to find someone!

Your body has basically been doing this work schedule thing all of its life, and so it won't fail to respond to it all again. This is your culture, and your country. This is what your roots are watered with. Denying it, or using the 'great travelling experience' as a reason for not being able to get back to work, I believe, is just an excuse for idleness. Theoretically, your experience should motivate you to work and do everything that you want to do. It'll all come back to you, so don't worry about it! In relation to what you've just done, it might seem like the worst option, but then this is where your 'itchy feet' come into the equation. They will help you to dream and relive memories. Every holiday from then on, if you can afford it, you'll be off. You'll certainly enjoy a more active life!

A wasted year?

Don't be ridiculous! Anyone who says that to you has obviously never done anything interesting in their life. How can taking time out having fun, exploring amazing countries, broadening your mind and doing whatever you want to do be a waste? As far as I'm concerned, a young person sat in an office for a year pushing paper clips around the desk earning money to spend on drinking binges... **is a waste**. No, I'm wrong... it's a **crime**! But that's just my opinion! Why get slated by others because I'm having fun in my life?

Jealousy. I suppose it all depends what you are on this planet for. You only have one chance in life... if you miss the boat – it's gone. **Game over**.

Chapter 2

Decisions

> ❛ *We pass this way but once. There is no normal, and there's no such thing as normal. There's you, and there's the rest. There's now and there's forever. Do as you damn well please!* ❜ **Billy Connolly**

Decisions, decisions

The obvious and most important place to start... making decisions! I'm a firm believer in making decisions and sticking to them, only changing them if you really have/want to. With decisions made, it is possible to go forward.

Do you know where you want to go?

No? Well I think it's about time you went off to a travel agent to have a little look around! If you've got lots of time before you go, make the most of it and get it all right. So go to the travel agents, pick up a few brochures on a few areas, and have a look at the pictures. Take them home and look at them over the weekend, or over a couple of days. This is actually the best and simplest way. It's true, the brochures will always show the best of the places, but it'll also give you a flavour of what's in store and definitely start to motivate you. If you're after adventure, you'll see photos of rapids, bungee-jumping, etc., along with offers and prices for them. You'll be surrounded by pictures of the Inca trails, Australian beaches, the Bush, Ayers Rock, Asian temples, waterfalls, caves, reefs, parrots, mountains, paradise, smiling faces, and young people having fun.

➤ **At this point you'll start to get fairly excited about the prospect of going, which is exactly what you want!**

What next?

After looking through the brochures, you'll have some idea about what you want to do, be it visiting just a few countries or loads, Inter-railing, or doing the 'full monty' of some kind of a round-the-world trip. Whatever you've decided, you should now take time to actually go and sit down with a travel agent to discuss a proposed trip. Within a day, your motivation will be given a huge kick as they will inform you of the relative costs of your trip, whether it is feasible, suggest other ideas/possibilities, and tell you when it is best to go. There is actually a book out called *Weather to Travel* (I've put it in the back

Ask about the weather cycles of where you want to go, as it may be worth going a month earlier/later so as to miss a monsoon/hurricane season, etc.

under '**Good books on the market**') which is a great book to leaf through and work out the best times to be in the countries you want to visit... just 10 minutes of study may be the answer to a really well-planned trip. Worth bearing in mind! By the time you eventually walk of out the door, you will have some definite ideas about where you really will be going, when you may be leaving, and how much it is going to cost, as well as a million and one other things buzzing around your head.

Student travel agents?

Travel agents are usually very obliging and will help you with your plans. If you find one that is particularly unhelpful, then walk away as there are loads of them around. Remember, you are about to put a lot of money in their pockets, so make sure you shop around. If you think positive and enjoy this first part, we've found that this generally sets you up for the trip.

You may not already be aware, but there are two types of travel agent available: 'holiday ones' and 'student ones'. Guess which one is right for you? That's right! You are probably more familiar with the Thomas Cooks and Lunn Polys of this world. These are the 'holiday ones' and the best ones to go to if you want to pay over-inflated prices and get the wrong sort of ticket for you.

'Student ones', on the other hand, are specialists in student travel or for anyone under the age of 26. Basically, they get all the cheap deals and, with the rise in the number of student travellers over the past few years, are getting some pretty wicked ones! You can get round-the-world tickets for as little as £650 nowadays. If this is the first time that you have found out that the tickets are this cheap, I hope I have just made your day!

Student travel agencies

There are a number of student travel agencies in the UK, so you should be able to find a branch near you. Most are situated in and around universities and student towns and will either be part of a large chain or an affiliation of one of them. The two largest are STA Travel and USIT Campus. (You'll find a list of branches on www.gapyear.com.) If you are under 26 or a student, you can get access to their low-cost fares which spank the fares you will be offered in High Street travel agents who specialise in holidays for nuclear families and the new breed of bungee-jumping, Gin & Tonic swigging 'Saga-louts'.

The general benefits of student travel agencies are:

- low-cost fares
- good service – as their staff tend to be experienced travellers who can offer first-hand advice
- offices around the world who can offer support and advice should you need to change your tickets.

See for yourself...

The best bet is to find out where your nearest student travel company is and go and have a look around. Look on the Internet to find the nearest one to you. See what it is like and get used to what they can offer you.

When you have an idea of where you want to go and when, head in and ask them all the questions you need to know about itineraries, flights, visas, insurance, prices, etc., and then go elsewhere and see if you can do better. I'd be very surprised if you can! But whatever you do, get some ideas buzzing round in your head so you can make some sort of start. From then on in, it's go, go, go, until you take off.

> **You need to start thinking about sitting down with a member of staff in a student travel agency for a chat and finding out what they can do for you.**

I now want to get you started

One of the most important things you need to do as soon as possible is to get a quote for your ticket. At least then you will have an idea as to how much it is going to cost you, a ball-park figure to aim at. The best way to do this is to plan a rough itinerary on a piece of paper, notes about where you want to go and, most importantly, when, and then head off to a student travel agent and get a quote. Whatever you do, don't just walk in there and say 'I want to go around the world!?!', as it is impossible for them to help you.

To help get you started, I have put together a bit of a guide to student travel companies below which you may well find useful. It will also give you a bit of a feel for who they are and what they have to offer. You may want to use it as a base to shop around? Whatever you do, I hope that for many of you this will be the first step on the road to the airport and the time of your life.

What do travel companies have to offer?

- The larger companies will have hundreds of branches in the UK and around the world, something you may want to look out for. This means that you should be able to go into a branch overseas if you have any problems with one of their tickets.
- They offer fully flexible tickets, so if you want to hang around for a while, you can (or if you want to get home earlier, you can). You are usually able to secure a ticket with as little as a £50 deposit.
- The majority run telesales teams, so if you can't get into a branch you can still get a quote.
- They also have International Travel Help Desks which understand that you are a young traveller travelling the world and can give you the advice and assistance you need.
- One of the best things they have to offer is their staff: thousands of well-travelled young people who will be able to share their experiences and advice with you. Great to chat to for inspiration and motivation.

Why do I get the best prices?

If you are a student or under 26 you can access their cheap fares, which they are able to negotiate with the airlines due to the enormous demand from their customers. They all have links with the top airlines and tour operators and, because they specialise in dealing with young travellers, offer all the round-the-world tickets and specialist fares you could ever need.

What if I don't want to go on my own?

There are all sorts of organised tours they can organise for you, from two-week excursions to the full monty 36-week overland expedition.

> ➤ **All the clichés are true: travel does broaden the mind, you are only young once, and memories are something that you'll always have, no matter what happens in the future. And, with fares for students and people under 26 falling all the time, your trip of a lifetime may never be more affordable. So don't hang around... do it!**

What are the advantages of a 'round-the-world' ticket?

The best thing about round-the-world tickets is that they are fully flexible and allow you to travel the world in your own time and at your own pace. Should you want to hang around in your beach hut for another month, lazing the days away in your hammock, you simply ring up and get it changed. And, as mentioned before, for those not having a good time or if you have to leave the country sharpish for some reason, your itinerary can be changed at a moment's notice. For my first trip, I took a round-the-world ticket and I would recommend it to anyone.

Round-the-world packages

What is a 'round-the-world' ticket then?

Well, you guessed it... as it says really. Think of it as a flight pass. You get a series of flights that literally take you around the world. For example, I did London to Los Angeles to Hawaii to Fiji, to Sydney, out of Perth, into Bali and then out of Bangkok back to London. You pretty much have to go to Los Angeles to go to any of the Pacific Islands (it is known as a Gateway City) and the 'into Sydney and out of Perth' and 'into Bali and out of Bangkok' both allowed me to fly into one airport/country, do a bit of overland travel and then fly out of another city/country. So all you need to do is work out the countries you would like to go to and roughly how long you would like to stay in each one. You will then have an itinerary worked out for you and a series of flights booked. No worries!

For a first-time 'Big Trip', or for any sort of big trip for that matter, these tickets are definitely seen as the best and safest things to buy, and they are perfectly suited to you. I took one and recommend them to everyone.

- The flights are already booked in advance, so you don't have to worry about organising them.
- If you want to stay longer in a country, simply ring the airline or contact your travel agent to change the dates of your flights (depending on validity of ticket and availablility of flights of course).
- The only thing you need to remember, which is fairly important, is to catch the flight(!). If you don't, your ticket may become invalid and be very difficult to sort out again. You may think that it's odd me mentioning this, but not getting to the airport on time, or just forgetting that you are meant to leave... have happened! The backpackers have then had all sorts of problems.
- Also you must remember to confirm your flights 72 hours in advance, as once you are away it is up to you to get in touch with the airline in case the flight times have changed.
- Get to the airport at least two hours before the plane is due to leave. I thought this was solely to do with giving the airline time to get you all on to the plane. However, I have been informed that it is in fact policy, and that if you don't turn up on time they do have the right not to take you (unlikely, but not worth the hassle of testing this theory out!).

If you hear people talk of round-the-world tickets saying that you are tied to flights, limited stays, etc., I'm afraid they're talking rubbish! Furthermore, if you have any problems or want/have to return home for some reason (even if you run out of money), you simply change the flights to fly you home as fast as you need to. Simple, eh?

Itinerary ideas

- Remember, all of these should be used as a guide to get you started and not the gospel truth.
- Remember also that most of these trips can be done in the opposite direction to either fit in with weather cycles (avoiding monsoon/typhoon/baboon periods) or to do the easy countries first to get you used to travelling before you do the more difficult ones – i.e. I did the USA and Australia before South-east Asia on my first trip.

The most popular round-the-world ticket is as follows:

London – Bangkok – Bali – Sydney – Auckland – Fiji – Los Angeles – London

This will cost you around £825 at the time of writing.

Want to see a bit more of South-east Asia? Brilliant – when you go to the travel agent ask about fitting in Cambodia, Vietnam and Laos before you get to Bangkok or, if you're doing it the other way round, ask about making them the last destinations before you head home. These countries are becoming more and more popular with backpackers and I for one have regretted not visiting them when I had the chance when I was out there. Yes they are a little bit more difficult to travel through, and yes there are a couple of dodgy areas – however there are thousands of backpackers out there now and the dodgy areas are easily avoided.

Want to do more Pacific Islands? To be honest the Pacific Islands are a little bit overrated. Yes you will dream of those palm-lined beaches, sun-tanned chicks in grass skirts and muscly adonises catching massive fish with their bare teeth, but in reality you will find it very 'the same' and a touch touristy. The best bet is to see if you can get a good deal with an airline that gives you the options of going to a few Pacific Islands and then getting off the beaten track. Great for topping up your suntan on your way out/back from Oz, for chilling on the beach or doing some scuba diving or surfing. However, also wicked for learning about the relaxed Pacific way of life, checking out some spectacular countryside and getting to meet some of the friendliest people on earth. Read up on the Cook Islands, the different Hawaiian islands, the thousands of Fijian Islands and French Polynesia and then go and chat to your travel agent to see what offers are around.

Want to see a bit of Central and South America? Very easy to bolt onto a round-the-world trip like the ones outlined above (simply extend your stopover in Los Angeles – the gateway to the Pacific Islands – and head south to Mexico, Guatemala etc.), but to be honest these areas warrant a trip by themselves.

London – Mexico City – surface Belize and Guatemala – Lima – surface Peru, Bolivia and Chile – Santiago – London

This is quite a long trip from Central America down through South America. Travelling through Central and South America can be a bit tricky at times, but the 'dangerous element' (as your granny/mum may see it) can be cut down by flying between countries and taking the more expensive (but quicker and more comfortable/air-conditioned) express buses. This trip will give you a great flavour of this amazing continent.

For a quick, simple Mayan, coral and Central American experience think about a nice loop, starting out in Mexico and overlanding it through Belize and

Guatemala and then back up to Mexico. More history and mind-blowing stuff than you could throw a sodding great stick at. Also, in Belize, the second-largest coral reef in the world – a great place to chill, swim with the fishes and learn to scuba dive (one of the cheapest places to do your PADI). Cuba is also a relatively short hop if you fancy checking out one of the fastest-growing destinations and smoking a real Cuban cigar the size of your heeeed!

After a bit of va va voom? Have a think about a visit to Brazil... why not time your trip so you land in Rio de Janeiro when the carnival is in town? A once-in-a-lifetime opportunity to be able to say 'I've been there' every time you see it on the telly for the rest of your life!

Millions of pink flamingos poncing around on a massive flat salt pan? That'll be Bolivia. *Machu Picchu?* That'll be Peru. *Mountains, desert and a once-in-a-lifetime opportunity to nip to the South Pole for lunch?* That'll be Chile! I think you can see what I am getting at here. Big continent with loads of weird and wonderful things. Very easy to fly in and out of all these countries and affordable too. Just bear in mind that you are talking large distances here, so it's essential you do your homework before you head to the travel agent!

I could go on all day about the different areas of the world, but I won't, as it's your job to do a bit of homework to find out where everything is and focus on what you want to do and when. Above are the usual variations of the bulk standard round-the-world ticket that I tend to be asked about. Wherever you want to go, when making decisions the advice is simple.

1. Be realistic – don't bite off more that you can chew.
2. If you can't do it all now, do it some another time – the next trip.
3. Build in flexibility (see below).
4. Make decisions about what you can realistically afford, not what your dreams want you to do. Better to spend two months really getting to see just Australia than four months rushing round the world not being able to do anything because you can't afford it. You have the rest of your life to see the friggin' world, so don't try to do it all at once!
5. Do your homework. Head onto gapyear.com and find out about what to do and where. Missing one of the greatest wonders of the world 'because you didn't know it was there' is just stooopid!

Build in flexibility

There is absolutely no point in rushing through fantastic countries just to catch a plane out on the other side. You'll end up missing all the good bits and experience absolutely nothing. When chatting to various foreigners I always hear stories of people visiting only London and then taking off again with a view that London typifies what England is all about. I can appreciate that a lot of them are simply flying through and so do not have any more time than a day for a quick 'whip around the capital' and a cup of tea with a hot buttered muffin in a Turkish-owned tea room/souvenir shop just off Trafalgar Square. Have they really seen England?... 'Why good lord NO old chap!' I can hear a lot of you saying... 'Blighty is more than just the clogged-up streets of Whitehall!' Very true, eh?

So why is it then that hundreds of backpackers every year disappear off thousands of miles around the world to Australia, land in Sydney, get a job, and stay there for 11 months? They then realise at this point what they are actually there for and so attempt to see Australia in a month, hurtling round the country by plane! Is Sydney Australia? I found at the end of the day that a city is just a city wherever you are in the world. Yes, they all have their attractions and their focal points... but if you go thousands of miles to see a country, you might as well have a look round it. By all means come back to Sydney to work, as it is a great place to work to earn money, but don't get stuck there (or anywhere else similar). You might as well be working at home... as all you've done is jump from one rat race to another.

Budget for the things that you really do want to do

Cairns, Australia: the home of bungee-jumping, rafting, scuba diving the Barrier Reef, etc., etc. Queenstown, New Zealand: one of the adventure capitals of the world, again with bungee-jumping, rafting, skydiving, rock climbing, rap jumping, jet boating, helicopter rides and the infamous 'Awesome Foursome'. If you are going to any of these places for 'adventure', do make sure that you budget your money to do all the things that you want to do. There is nothing worse than getting to a place like this where everyone else is doing all the things that you long to do... except you, because you've basically wasted it in big drinking sessions on the way up the coast. So do try and think about these things ahead of time, and budget accordingly.

Finally, on the flexibility front, by budgeting, planning and doing everything that you want to do, you should have an absolutely fantastic time. As more and more countries are opening up and becoming more accessible to backpackers than ever before, the packages sold by the travel agents are becoming better and better. You can now go virtually anywhere you want to... so make sure that you do! There is no point in rushing your way around the world or through countries. You have all this time ahead of you, so make the most of it... as it may not happen again... ever.

So, you think you've found the ideal package?

Before this stage, everything is just talk. As my brother Mat once said, 'In this world there are "doers" and "talkers".' I'm a 'doer', and the fact that you're

A good tip here is buy early. By doing this it reduces the option of cancelling (as many have been known to 'bottle it' at the last moment), and you know then that you really are going, as you have a date and time. In fact, once you've paid for it... you're virtually there.

reading this means that you are too... so don't blow it at the last minute and become a 'talker'! Once you've bought the ticket you'll find it's plain sailing from here on in. Quite simply, if you need money to finance your trip you now have a date to earn it all by, hence starting early is always a good idea. If you're going with a friend you'll also have the added incentive of not letting him or her down. For myself, January 7th was the big 'D Day', aged 18. I needed the money and so took every shift possible at McDonald's, working round the clock and saving every single penny.

Now you have a date to aim at

From this point you'll be able to organise your time properly. Therefore it's now time to buy essentials like backpacks, sleeping bags, tents, etc.... you may even find that your birthday, Christmas, or even both fall in between the time you buy your ticket and go. So why not surprise those caring relatives of yours by actually asking for something useful for your travels... and not another pair of socks that you're never going to wear and that are going to go to the back of the drawer! Little things such as a small torch, combination padlock, travel saucepan, etc. (see Packing), which you will find invaluable, but which added expense you could do without.

Your 'Rellies' will then think that they are helping you on your way, and you in turn can allow them to believe that they have performed this wondrous deed by mentioning in their postcard about how you're finding it odd *not wearing any socks out in Peru*, but how the torch they gave you saved you (and your friends) from imminent danger when you got lost in some caves in the mountains... when in fact you'll probably find it invaluable

Be positive and book early... buy the ticket and think about where you are going, what you are doing, how you will afford it, what your budget is, and how you are going to plan it all.

helping everyone find their way back to the hostel after a great night out, or for seeing turtles hatching on the beach, or something as mundane or trivial as that! Well, I'm sure you know by now what I'm going to say! Time for another…

What do I see as the key?

You'll suddenly find that you'll take more of an interest in the holiday programmes on TV, travel supplements in the paper and novels on people's travelling experiences, etc. You'll hear yourself saying things like 'I'm off there!', 'That's where I'm going!'… but be careful not to drive too many people nuts! Unfortunately you'll come up against a lot of jealousy, but don't let it put you off. If they wanted to do it they would have done it already. They're 'talkers' and just don't like seeing others have the guts to do something they'd never have the nerve to do themselves… you're doing it, so good for you!

However, just general 'chatter' about your impending trip will really excite you even more about the whole thing. But at the same time you will be nervous, of course you will, you'd be daft to deny it. Before the Canadian trip, due to lack of money/idea about what I was about to do I was nervous right up to the departure… although I tried to let my friends see that I wasn't (male macho image and all that!). But once you are on your way, on the plane, boat, or in the car, a real sense of adventure and nervous excitement takes over… you're off, and there's no going back! This is of course totally untrue, as if ever you don't enjoy it (unlikely) or feel you've had enough for whatever reason… you can easily come home. There is no shame in doing that; at least you've given it a go.

> ➤ **If you are your own person, then you can go wherever, or do whatever you want… can't you?**

What did we all use for motivation?

Why do you want to know this? Well, maybe you'd like to see how much you're now in the same situation as a lot of other people.

- Well… **boredom** was actually the biggest factor amongst us all. Colin, for example, was on the dole before he left… unmotivated, in need of a change, and desperate to get out of England for a while. 'It just seemed like a good idea at the time!'
- Have you been studying 'hard' for a few years? (Or maybe I should just say have you been studying?)
- Always doing the same thing? Always going to the same places?… seeing the same people, talking about the same thing? Same same same same same. Arghhhhhhhhhhhhhhh!

What is your motivation?

- Or maybe you're in a job and you're now at a point where the novelty has worn off? You always seem to be working, everything is the same, and you seem to have dropped into a 'live to work, work to live' routine.
- **You're young... you have the chance to break from this... so do it before it's too late.**

Take hold of your life... now!

Whenever I've said something to others along these lines about getting bogged down in work, the reaction always seems to be **'well that's life Tom!'**... usually said to me by older generations. However, things have changed since their day, and I'm sorry **but that is not life**! Fifteen years ago it was fairly uncommon for young people to take time out and travel the world; these were experiences only had by those in the armed forces who had to serve overseas, or people in shipping, the Foreign Office, etc. The 'normal routine' therefore was (and still is if you think about it) to get qualifications, get a job, settle down, and then do your travelling over a long period of time in a series of two-week holidays, where you often get to see nothing more than the hotel, the pool, and a few restaurants and beaches... Once you hit your late 20s and above, you start to have commitments; you can't just up and leave with only a moment's notice. This is why so many of the people that I've met on my travels have encouraged me, always telling me about how they missed out when they were young.

So don't miss out, life is what you make of it. You're going to have plenty of years to settle down to a job, enter the 'rat race', etc. One year in your life of having fun and doing everything that you want is only going to benefit you (as I've said before... what is the difference between working for 43 years and 44 years?... Isn't it great being able to look at things from a different angle)... **so GO!**

Additional planning tips

Other motivators?... well everything from:

- Adventure – if you want to be adventurous, go for it, there will never be a better time.
- Adrenalin – I have bungee-jumped, rafted, sky dived and rap jumped, scuba dived, and loved every single second of each one. If you're daft enough to want to do silly stuff like this that you will remember for the rest of your life, there's some wicked stuff out there for you – so don't miss out and regret it.
- Curiosity – the best thing about the world is discovering it. Why do some South American tribes stick a washing-up bowl in their bottom lip? Why do the Swiss not have a sense of humour? Find out!
- 'Discovering yourself' – and putting things in perspective. It is such a great feeling to realise that you are actually alive and that, believe it or not, 'life is great'. Money? Materialism? All the stuff you think is important right now, when you come back you won't give a flying Scooby about...
- **Research – into the countries** you are about to visit is quite a cool thing to do, i.e. find out about their capitals, the seasons, temperatures, what they produce, etc. Improves your 'Trivial Pursuit' knowledge and may help you with the difficult questions at the serious money stage of 'Who wants to be a millionaire?'.
- The **political situation** – will things be changing while you are there? I have been in countries at the time of elections, an awesome thing to see as the country literally changes around you. However, if you are visiting some countries where the political situation resembles the morning after a particularly turbulent vindaloo, this is essential. The Foreign Office website www.fco.gov.uk is an absolute 'must visit' as soon as you have a

rough idea of where you want to go; their Know Before You Go Campaign is an essential read, found at www.fco.gov.uk/knowbeforeyougo. Great name for a campaign, eh?!

- **Major events** – may be happening around the time that you are visiting a place, and you may be able to coincide your visit accordingly, e.g. South East Asian Olympics, elections, Australia Day, Independence Day, national festivals, etc.

All of this tends to help build the excitement, makes your trip more eventful, and even helps to give you a broader knowledge and an understanding of events that are happening on the other side of the world. In Tony's own words:

➤ 'You've got to remember that the rest of the world has far more to offer than what can be found on your doorstep'... something that I think that a lot of us tend to forget, as we get absorbed into our own little worlds and everything that revolves just around us.

Did I hear someone say 'rat race'?

Chapter 3

Packing

> ' A traveller must have a falcon's eye, an ass's ear, an
> ape's face, a merchant's words, a camel's back, a
> hog's mouth, and a stag's legs '
>
> **English Proverb (late 16th century)**

... a fair description of one of my drunken snogs!

AARRRGGHHHH!!

Do you really need it?

Another essential chapter, but again mostly common sense. Picture the scenario, a friend of mine Tim, off to Australia... does he really need to take his favourite new pair of Cat boots? Of course, I knew that he wanted to impress the ladies, but weighing about a kilo it's a lot to take in your backpack (as well as the bulkiness of them). If you are going to hot countries, think hot! Indeed there may well be times when you want to go hiking (Tim's excuse), but you will invariably find that you will be able to hire these things on site, or that a multi-purpose pair of strong trainers or Desert Boots may do the trick... you'll find everyone's a bit less fashion conscious when they're travelling. In fact, Tony – possibly one of the vainest people this side of the Equator – was even known to wear a cagoule when the rain came down, although I was sworn to secrecy at the time! DOH!... secret's out!

What is a good backpack?

The most important tip is to **PACK LIGHT, leave home with a half-empty backpack** if possible... because by the time you return, it will be weighing 10 times the original weight and bursting at the seams with all the 'bits and pieces' that you've acquired along the way. This is why it really is essential to **buy yourself a decent backpack** if you don't already have one. With the amount of travelling, carrying and general 'lumping around' that you will be doing, a comfortable backpack is essential. You've got to remember that this will be your personal 'caravan' for a long period, and if it falls apart (like mine did in Canada), it will cause you nothing but unnecessary aggro all the way round. A capacity of 65 litres is usually sufficient, with some of the 'petite' amongst us opting for the 55 litre.

There are two types of backpack that you need to check out to decide which is the best for you. For a simple explanation I'll call them '**The normal one**' and the '**One that converts into a holdall/suitcase**'.

The normal one – is the one you have probably seen before. It loads from the top, has two sections (a top half and a bottom half), side pockets, loads of toggles and zips and the option of an adjustable backsystem and bars that give it support and strength when it is bursting at the seams with all the useless crap you will pick up along the way (remember you will somehow be drawn to buying a toothpick holder 'as an interesting table ornament' for your mum, handcarved by a Khazakstani monk for about 25p, which is about the size and weight of a standard coffee table... you think I'm joking, right!).

The '**One that converts into a holdall/suitcase**' – I've kinda given you a clue in the title. A great invention, very popular with backpackers. If you've never seen one, picture the normal backpack in your mind and stick a daypack on its back (a small backpack which zips off), then lie the whole pack on its side and open the zip like a suitcase – which means you can load it up like a suitcase. The beauty is that you can either wear it like a normal backpack or, when it is on its side, zip the shoulder straps away and then carry it like a holdall/suitcase. This can sometimes help you at borders and airports where you might be pulled over as a backpacker – sort of helps to make you look respectable. *Still don't know what I'm talking about? Don't worry – examples of these two types of backpacks can be found in the gapyearshop.com*

When you get your backpack, put loads of stuff in it to feel what it is like with a bit of weight in – preferably at the point of purchase if you are buying it in a shop. Then go for a long walk with it on, taking time to adjust it and find the comfortable positioning and balance for you. If it doesn't feel right then change it. You are going to be carrying this thing around with you all the time, so you need to get the right one for you. If you are excessively tall, short, fat or thin, then you may want to look at a backpack with an adjustable back system which allows you to find the right balance and centre of gravity – it will stop you injuring your back when the weight of the toothpick holder starts to kick in!

Some questions you might like to think about: * Is it comfortable? * How do I adjust it? * How am I meant to pack it? – weight at the top/bottom? – Where should my sleeping bag go? (to be accessed daily) * Does it have reinforcers to stop it bulging when it gets full? * Could it possibly leak? – Should I seal it? * Can I make the bag secure? – Can the zips be padlocked together? – Are the holes in the zips wide enough for the padlock to go through? * Why is this model cheaper than the rest? (if word 'quality' appears in the answer, beware!) * I have a bad back/a damaged shoulder/am pregnant/ have three arms – which one is best suited to me?

YOU'VE GOTTA GET A GOOD ONE. I can't hammer this point home enough. You are a 'backpacker' after all... your job is to have a pack – on your back! Nuff said.

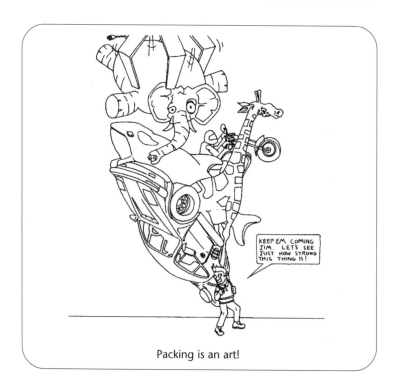

Packing is an art!

What to take?

Well... I did a little survey of my group of contributors and it was amazing how most of us came up with the same things. But when you think about it, it's not too surprising, as we now all know to keep it light and pack only the bare essentials. The following is therefore an idea of some of our contents to give you an idea of what you may be forgetting, and also to make you think whether you do need to take that 'Best of Eric Clapton' CD on the off-chance that you find a CD player somewhere in Nepal so that you can listen to Layla and remind yourself of a class night with your best mate two summers ago! There are also a few other 'bits and bobs' you may think are a good idea to take:

ESSENTIAL

Address book + pens

You are going to meet all sorts of people who you will want to keep in touch with. Get a compact address book, but look for one with a bit of room to write stuff in, as a few notes about the person will help you to remember them. It is always useful to carry your own pens, but cheap plastic ones break easily. Cheap solid ones and you're sorted.

Alarm clock
It is so easy to miss flights, buses, tours, sunrises and other important stuff through over-sleeping. Get a solid one with a good ring tone, so it will still wake you up four months into its trip despite looking like it has done 10 rounds with Mike Tyson.

Backpack
As above. Make sure you invest in a decent one. It will last you years and you'll use it loads, so it will be well worth the money you will pay.

Camera + film
Photography is covered later on (see page 166). It depends what sort of photos you're after as to what camera and film you take. Good cameras can be expensive to buy, look after and replace (check your insurance fully to see that you are covered), but worth it if you want awesome shots. For everyday good photos a compact camera, maybe with a small zoom, shouldn't be too expensive and will help you get the shots you want. Cheap cameras will more than likely give you cheap shots. Think robust and solid. Why not try out different films – I got some great black and white pics once with my first go.

Candles
Have always used them when I've had them. Awesome for camping. A fire hazard, so please be careful.

Daypack (see page 33)

Knife/fork/spoon set
I have always found mine invaluable, especially in hostels when all the cutlery has gone, for camping or when I am on the move and need a knife, fork or spoon to eat with. Your call. But don't forget that since the September 11th tragedy in New York, almost all airlines now ban (and search for) any sharp objects, including knives and forks, in your carry-on luggage. Pack your knife/fork/spoon set in into your checked luggage bound for the airplane's hold.

Matches/lighter
Essential. Normally have a couple of each for lighting fires, mosquito coils, candles, etc.

Pack of cards
Awesome accessory at airports, waiting for buses, late nights in hostels, for making friends – card games, like music, cross all international languages. Learn a couple of card tricks and games before you head off.

Padlocks (+ chain?) for backpack
Make you feel more confident about leaving your bag and are fairly essential when you think there are thieves about. Don't want the hassle of keys? Get a combination padlock.

Peg-free washing line
Chances are you've never heard of one of these before. For anyone that knows me you will be aware that I would be prepared to marry the inventor of this gadget and have their children if humanly possible. Twisted elastic with hooks at the end. Allows you to dry your pants virtually anywhere by trapping them in the twisted elastic. You too will fall in love with such a random item.

Penknife + attachments
If you have never used one before you will most certainly use one on your travels. For cutting things, mending things and the tin opener attachment once saved my arse once when I had a tin of pineapple, a mouth as dry as a camel's backside and not a tin opener in sight. Marvellous gadget. Invented by the Swiss? Bear in mind that due to increased airline security measures, you can't take this on the plane with you as carry-on luggage. Pack it into your checked luggage, not your carry-on.

Plastic bags
- Small ones with a seal... you'll be amazed how often they come in handy, especially keeping things dry, or preventing wet/leaky things wetting everything else.
- Shopping ones, e.g. Tesco... you'll find that it takes a long time to get things dry, so these are ideal to put wet things in, and for separating your items in your backpack.

Sewing kit
Yet again, essential. You will thank your lucky stars that you have it if ever you need to use it. Everything from putting buttons on trousers to sewing limbs back on bodies – only kidding, but an enduring image.

Sleeping bag
Check for the climate that you are going to and what 'season' bag you'll need. Some hot countries get very cold at night... as Colin found to his peril in Zimbabwe. Be safe – get a warm one. A two/three season should be adequate, three to four for extremely low temperatures.

Sleeping sheet
Often required in hostels as they don't like sleeping bags on the bed. (The sleeping bags could be full of bugs and crud where backpackers may have slept in them on beaches, round a camp fire etc.) Basically, they are standard cotton sheets sewn together to make a sleeping bag liner. You need one, so get one!

Small hairbrush/comb
Again, get a strong one that can go anywhere with you and will last the pace.

Small purse/wallet
On the road it isn't very practical to carry loose change around in your pockets, especially in countries where you get just over 12 million ChuiMui to the pound! It is worth finding a small purse/wallet that can get quite full of stuff but will still shut and can be carried around. Hard-wearing with a tough zip that won't fall apart the minute you stick it near water, dust or the like.

You also need a 'dummy wallet' to carry around with you which has a few dollars and valueless items in it. Should some ****** decide to relieve you of your valuables you simply hand over the dummy wallet – if they feel they have something they are more likely to do a runner than cause you more grief.

Small torch
Small so it can be hidden away, but powerful enough so it can actually be used. Maglites are good, solid and powerful; there are luminous ones that glow in the dark, and funky little ones that can be used as a lantern or a head lamp.

Sunglasses – cheap ones!
If Jurgen from Germany's fat backside sits on your best sunnies whilst out watching dolphins, not only will your magical moment be lost, but also you may well find yourself out of pocket. Expensive glasses also attract thieving hands. The sun is a lot stronger overseas than here, especially in Southern Hemisphere or Equatorial regions, so you need a pair that do the job more than score you a date on the beach.

Synthetic drawstring bags
- Again, ideal for dirty washing and as a separate bag for everyday use.

Toilet paper and tissues (flat pack)
When that moment arrives when you remember that you have these little life-savers tucked away in a dry safe place in your backpack, you'll thank me for reminding you to pack them. Curried goat is not all it is cracked up to be!

Towels
- Your main one shouldn't be too big or too thick. You are going to have problems getting it dry, especially when you are on the move, so air/wash it as often as possible to stop it smelling like a rancid goat.
- It is often a good idea to take a small hand towel as well. This can be carried in your day bag and will come in handy for a lot of things... as a pillow/head rest, for drying yourself when your backpack isn't around, etc.

- Pack towel. You may not have come across one of these, another beauty bit of kit. A small towel made of ultra-absorbent material that you use to get most of the water off you to save soaking your main towel. Absorbs loads of water and dries dead quick. Highly recommended.

Travel saucepan

- Small, closes shut so you can store things in it when you travel, and perfect size for whipping up a meal for yourself... eat out of it and save on washing up! Mine is the veteran of many a sausage casserole and a handy bowl for my Weetabix in the morning...

Travel wash

- Concentrated washing gel. A fantastic little item which lets you wash your clothes in hot or cold water. When your socks turn to cheddar, in both consistency, smell and most probably taste, a drop of this in a bucket of cold water, five minutes of grinding and they will be ready for another two months' use!

Universal sink plug

Similar to the peg-free washing line, this is another bit of kit I love. Sad, yes... but it makes me happy all the same. I love it because it is so simple, yet so useful. I use them at home. Blocks holes for washing clothes, you, plates etc., etc. Get one.

Washbag

- Full of the usual rubbish; I'm sure I don't have to remind you to take your toothbrush. However, things like tweezers, small pair of scissors (usually in first aid kit), small scrubbing brush, and best of all... nail clippers can be invaluable.
- For example, nail clippers to me are vital. They always have been. Used to cut everything apart from nails – removing objects from feet/body that shouldn't be there, cutting things... basically, I reckon I could perform a minor heart operation with them if the need arose. Invaluable! As I've mentioned a couple of times already, remember though, that due to the recent increase in airline security, you won't be able to take sharp metal objects on a plane in carry-on luggage. Check with your airline before your pack, but regulations normally include nail-clippers and could mean a re-pack by the check-in desk.
- If possible, get a washbag which rolls up (so you can get more in) and with a swivel hook in the top so you can hang it up in the shower or on the back of doors – saves launching it into the pool of stagnant water that

sometimes collects on the shower floor. It also allows you to hook it up to dry. Clear sides are good for finding stuff without opening the bag, and solid zips and a strong, waterproof material are vital. Most will split and, as this is one of your most used bits of kit, make sure you get a good 'un.

VITAL

Condoms

- Condoms are free at Family Planning, and are for sale at all chemists and even at some petrol stations now. (They'll soon be free with every £20 of unleaded no doubt!)
- Should be carried now by both men and women as it is the 'responsible thing to do'. Someone else may need them even if you don't at that moment. And if you don't use these fellas then you're a plank. You're going to have a lot of fun on your travels – it certainly opened my eyes to a whole pile of stuff – but you need to be careful right? There are some hotspots on the backpacker trail where STDs (Sexually Transmitted Diseases for those who don't know) are rife... and unless you want someone to stick an umbrella up/down your sensitive bits for a 'bit of a scrape' – or even worse catch something you want to leave out there (yup – I'm talking about AIDS from hetrosexual backpackers having sex) – you'll do the right thing. Me? I want to live to a ripe old age with all my pink bits intact. You? Your call.

Contact lenses

- Make sure that you have enough solution, protein tablets, etc.
- It's also worth having a pair of glasses as well (can be made up dead cheaply now, so not as expensive as you may think) as there may be times when it is impossible to wear lenses.

Driving licence

- Home/normal licence – make sure it is fully up to date and has the correct address on it. If you have a new version with the photo card, ensure that you take all the paperwork with you as well. The photocard is very useful as ID, especially in countries where it is law to carry around photo ID.
- You can also get an International Driving Licence which is very useful to have. Head to any branch of the AA (they are in most High Streets if you haven't spotted them already) and you can pick one up on the spot for about £5. It will act as ID and is also recognised around the world.

E111 – your health document

Essential if in Europe as it gives you medical cover and assistance and may be useful elsewhere. You can pick these up from your local Post Office but be aware that it doesn't cover you for everything, so you need to make sure your insurance covers you fully. I would recommend you get one of these anyway – I have always had one.

Finances (see 'Money and finances' on page 111)

- money
- travellers' cheques
- credit cards.

ID Cards

- It is vital that you carry as much ID with you as you can, as it may come in handy, not just for blagging but possibly in an emergency. Being able to prove that you are a student (for discounts), a tourist, a particular nationality or a certain age will be useful many many times during your trip. A variety of IDs mean that you can pull the right one out at the right moment. Most people overseas will have no idea what it is anyway and if they are merely asking for it so they can tick a box on a form or let you through a door, then a little bit of blagging with it will get you miles! Never ever let any bureaucratic nonsense get in your way... you can ALWAYS get round it.
- If you are a student make sure you carry an International Student Identity Card (ISIC card) as proof of student status, as in many places it may entitle you to a discount... something you should get in the habit of asking for everywhere – if you don't ask, you don't get! However, with the amount of fakes on the market (can be bought out in Thailand for about £5, bought by people under the age of 21 so they can drink in America... allegedly... of course I don't know anything about this!), some people have been known to turn the ISIC card down, so have your other ID at the ready.
- Other ID? 'Proof of Age Card', photocard with your domestic driving licence, school/college/university cards, a photocopy of your birth certificate all help to make any checks or paperwork go a lot quicker.

Passport!

You'd be surprised how many people forget! Make sure it is valid for the whole period you are away, and that you have all the necessary visas, or you're going to have serious problems later on – see also the passport section in '**Tips, hints and problems**' on page 165.

➤ NB: ensure it is signed and has the correct address on it.

Do you have dual nationality?

If yes, then you are an extremely lucky so-and-so, as you may be able to avoid queues, and be able to work in countries where many others can't. It is advisable therefore to get both passports up to date, and use the full benefit of them.

Passport photos
It's worth having a few with you kept in a nice dry place, often needed for temporary visas, permits, ID cards, etc. Try and make them look as respectable as possible – beards, hung-over expressions, scanty clothes and more piercings than an overenthusiastic acupuncturist may count against you. Look smart – will get you miles.

Before you head off, set up an account with a web-based email service; most of the big portals provide free email accounts – try Yahoo! (www.yahoo.com) or Lycos! (www.lycos.co.uk). Send an email to yourself and your parents before you head off, with all your important details on it and save it in your Inbox so you can get to it from an Internet café. Your parents will also be able to reach it quickly. If they are scared of technology and have not allowed the Information Superhighway up the drive, send copies to their friends who have actually joined the 21st century and who can look after this information for them.

Photocopies
- Make photocopies of all essential documents. You should keep two sets and give another set to your parents or extremely close friends who should keep them in a safe place for a time when you are going to ring at 4am to get your insurance reference number! (Don't tell them this though!!) Make sure they do something to remember where the documents are; if this paperwork is needed, they will need to find it quickly. Photocopy your passport, air tickets, insurance documents, credit cards and emergency numbers, travellers' cheques numbers, etc. Everything which is anything to do with your trip and which may be of use should you lose everything. (It doesn't really matter if you lose the physical items, as long as you have reference numbers, phone numbers to call, etc., which will get you replacements.)

- It's important to keep separate copies in your backpack and day bag, so if one gets lost, you're all right Jack!
- Medical: it's important to have copies of your GP's address, your medical insurance documents, evidence of jabs, blood group, allergies, etc., especially if you are allergic to something like Penicillin + **let others you travel with know.**

References

You need to take personal references and work references if you have them; especially useful for getting bar work, silver service waiting, etc., if you have the experience. My McDonald's reference from all the hours I worked earning the cash for my trip helped me find work in McDonald's in Australia. It is also a good idea to take evidence of qualifications such as GCSEs, 'A' levels, degree and anything else you think may be of interest.

Sanitary towels and tampons

Unfortunately for the girls these are not free at the family planning, and it is wise to stock up. As mentioned in the chapter **Female solo**, sanitary towels and tampons are available just about everywhere, although they won't necessarily be the slim, comfortable items that you usually use.

Suncream + sunblock

I took sun factor 6 because I usually use 4 maximum, 2 or tanning oil (as I have fairly olive skin). Unfortunately, in Fiji the sun was a LOT hotter than I was used to, and so I fried really badly... something to do with the ozone layer I think! So be prepared. You'll tan just as well with a 15, and besides you've got plenty of time to get a tan if you want one. If you've got fair skin you can even slap on factor 60 and get a tan in really hot sun! It's no longer a quick two weeks in the Costa del Sol with the family or the lads'/lassies' beano to Ibiza, although you'll find the excitement and heat of both up the east coast of Australia, and in the backpacker havens of Thailand!

Skin cancer is a thing no one likes to talk about and it is something young people think we are immune to. I changed my mind after meeting Australians who have had these things cut out of their arms, legs and faces. Don't want to scare you, just want you to take the issue seriously. It can kill you (even here in the UK), but not if you use adequate protection. You will tan just as well with a 15 or even a 30 or 40 – so whack it on at all times.

Sterilised kits and medical kits

These are both so important that they need their own little section. You need to make sure you get a decent one of both of these, as they are the two most important bits of kit that go in your backpack aside from your favourite pair of lucky pants and 'Pooky' your bestest friend/teddy bear/soul mate.

'Sterilised kit' – a sterilised needle kit

- Something you have probably never come across, but an essential bit of travel kit. I was a bit scared to take one (I have a massive fear of needles), but knew that it was important to have the kit. Basically it is a sealed, sterilised pack that contains needles and other stuff a doctor may need if a few repairs are needed on your bodywork. It is essential that you take one and store it in a place where it can be whipped out and given to a doctor in the event of an emergency. It means that your needles can be used in places where the safety of such items can't be assured. Ethically it is also important to take one, as you may be in a country with scarce local resources which, as a visitor to the country, you shouldn't use up.

Medical kit

- Another essential item. Shop around and make sure you get a good one which is full of all the things you need. There are some pretty poor ones around, especially the small compact ones which may look attractive to you to save space in your backpack but have nothing really useful, i.e. sharp scissors, iodine, proper bandages, plasters, rehydrate, etc. Note that I have called it a 'medical kit' as opposed to a 'first aid kit' – so you need to get one that will enable you to treat yourself whilst you are on the road. Many first aid kits exist to treat paper cuts in offices... so make sure you get one you are happy with.

Evidence of injections

- Always advisable to keep in a safe place, again photocopies should be with you and your parents. Stuff like this can always be faxed to the relevant person when asked for.

'The runs', 'galloping trots', or more politely... 'traveller's tummy'. Imodium tablets do the business better than an Albanian shot putter with an industrial mallet and a cork! Take them with you in your first aid kit, but be wary about letting some of the infection out before plugging it up, as it can be very dangerous. Remember to re-hydrate – 'Rehydrate' or flat Coke drunk slowly does the job.

These medical kits and documents should be kept in an easily accessible place so they can be whipped out in an emergency, not only for yourself but also for other people. But check with your airline before your pack; regulations could now prevent you from taking a medical kit or even some medical supplies in your carry-on bag (they'll be accepted in checked-luggage). The regulations could cover your medical supplies (for example, if you need to take an inhaler for asthma or syringes for diabeties).

DAYPACK

This is so much of an essential item that it warrants a paragraph of its own. It is advisable to have a daypack for a number of reasons.

- By getting one that you can padlock, or secure in some way, you can use it as your own personal 'safe' and keep all your most important items in it, such as your passport, money, tickets, documents, etc. I find that it's useful to put all of these inside a money belt inside the bag.
- You'll find that with all these things in one small bag, you'll never let it out of your sight. Also, you'll get used to always putting it in secure places wherever you end up, so you'll always have peace of mind.
- The daypack is also useful for the travelling part of the trip when you are on trains, buses, planes and long car journeys. If you have a small towel and washbag in there you can use it to freshen up, or for a cushion on those all too long and tedious bus/train rides. If you are in the airport and the plane is delayed and your luggage has gone through, it can be a life saver to have things like a washbag, books, food, cards, spare pants, etc. with you.

What sort of bag?

- Well, many like to take one of those little backpacks as they're nice and comfortable to wear. You need to think about carrying this as well as your backpack (which of course will be on your back). To be honest, most of them are pretty much the same; just make sure that it is a good, strong material, has good stitching, strong zips and is waterproof.
- Many backpacks now have daypacks attached 'all-in-one', as described earlier on in this section in the backpack section. Basically these are backpacks which can have their straps zipped away, be put on their side and turned into a holdall/suitcase. These are extremely popular with backpackers and have the added bonus of a daypack attached to them (giving added space to the backpack) which can be removed and used separately as a daypack. However, if it is a 65-litre backpack with one of these bags on the back, do have a think because this will reduce the 'main backpack' to about a 55-litre capacity, as the daypack makes up the other 10 litres of the 65 litres. You need to work out if this is too small.

- The other option is a small holdall or backpack which can be collapsed and zipped up flat into virtually nothing. I have always used one of these and find them extremely useful.

Either of these are ideal as they can easily be put away into your backpack or attached back on to your backpack when not needed.

OPTIONAL

Address cards (see 'Tips, hints and problems', page 142)
- Pop a couple in your backpack – handy if your bag gets lost, means it will eventually come back to you!
- Get some personalised ones made up, great to swap (but easy to lose).

Battery shaver
How hairy are you? Sometimes they work for you, others have to be content with disposables… if so, take enough if you're not visiting a developed country for a while. Or maybe you're looking forward to cultivating that long awaited beard?… Chance to do it!

Black marker pen
You'd be surprised where this comes in useful. Things like marking food bags when you put them in the communal fridges, essential for hitch-hiking and generally for marking anything else that I can't think of right now. I love them… but then I have always been a bit odd!

Diary
I always keep diaries of my travels! Great to read later on, but they also help to remember names of places and friends for future reference. Highly recommended, even for those of you who wouldn't ordinarily think of doing it.

Inflatable neck pillow
If you've got one and find it comfortable to use, why not take it? It packs away to nothing and is dead useful on those long journeys.

Mosquito net and insect repellent
You'll need these if you're travelling to really hot countries where they're required. Vital in areas with malaria.

Multi vitamins
Worth getting a batch of them to supplement your diet, especially in areas where your eating habits may change/be a bit dodgy (i.e. it really is a 'Hot Dog'!).

Personal alarm (see 'Tips, hints and problems', Protection)
Great little gadget, not only for the girls lads. Can be used for protection on the street, as a door guard, bag alarm. Cheap and small, but one day you may

be glad that you decided to take one. Awesome for peace of mind and may just save your bacon!

Poncho

The day the heavens open and the ensuing monsoon attempts to turn you into a fish you will be glad you have one of these. I remember my first tropical storm, something we don't get many of in Suffolk. I left the tent to head for the shower block. 15 seconds later, mid-stride, it started. 10 seconds later and with the contents of the Niagara Falls dumped on my head, it stopped and the sun came out. Tony popped his head out the tent with the expression of 'What the **** was that?' and then died laughing at my drenched, battered body halfway between the tent and the shower block. Not fashionable, but cheap and you WILL use it to cover yourself, your backpack, to make a shelter, to sit on... we even repaired our tent with it! Get one and store it somewhere where it can be whipped out in a hurry.

Roll mat

Essential if taking a tent as you'll find the ground very hard; also very handy for sitting on when waiting for buses, on beaches and also for helping your backpack to stand up (stabilisers!)

Telecommunication card (see 'Keeping in touch' on page 48)

There are loads of telecommunication companies out there that can offer you a good cheap service. With my brother out in Australia now, I use various ones which allow me to call him for as little as 5p per minute, as opposed to £138 per minute with BT (I jest of course about the BT price, but it may feel like it when the bill comes through with the sum equivalent to a lottery win in the 'Total you have to pay' section!).

You need to check out two types of telecommunication:

1. An account which your mum and dad can use from their phone at home – there are loads of them, for example where they pay £20/£30 up front and then use it as an account which needs topping up every now and then. They will get cheap international calls so all you have to do is get to a phone which will take incoming calls – arrange a time by email, send them the number and then wait for the call.

2. Your own account which stays with you while you travel around. You hook up to a network which gives you cheap calls so you can call home, mates etc.

BT chargecards are extremely expensive, so watch out for that. If you do go for the chargecard option, ensure that you get it so it can only dial one number, i.e. your parents' – so if it does get nicked, the thief won't be able to do anything with it.

Tent (see 'Tips, hints and problems', Camping)

If travelling solo or with a friend, a tent can turn out to be cheap to live in. I had never used one before my first trip and now I have taken one on a couple of trips. The ones with the bendy frames are the best – just chuck it at the ground and it sort of puts itself up – easy! They are light, easy to put away in a hurry and stronger than they look. Can be a great laugh and an awesome way to meet the locals and see a bit of the countryside or bush. Do take local advice about where to camp, the sort of animals that might want to bed down with you and the safe places to pitch it. Downtown LA, outside the bus station is a bad place. In a campsite overlooking a beautiful beach with rolling surf – is a good place. That sort of thing...

Tubigrip

You know, the stuff you can put on most parts of your body when you have an injury. A girl in Australia once showed me how she wears it at the top of her thigh under her shorts as a way of concealing her money. As it is tight you can hide notes in it safely. It was such a good idea that I asked her to show me it again later (after I had had a few beers)... unfortunately all I got was a slap!

Walkman/CD-player + music

- Good idea to have for those long journeys that you may be going on, especially good when you want to shut out irritating people/old grannies who want to gas about random subjects for the entirety of the trip. However, the downside is things like having to look after it (damp/being knocked around/damage), and if it is a nice one... 'making sure that it doesn't walk man!' (bad joke, but I really don't care!), making sure that no one nicks it.

- Great for letting other people listen to what sort of music we have over here, and vice-versa... conversational pieces! Music crosses all international barriers and all that. Kinda freaky sometimes having a Pidgin English conversation about Robbie Williams with a Swede, two Danes, a Japanese guy, a German, three French and two Swiss lassies...

Waterproof pouch

- A good bit of kit. In hot countries it can stop sweat moulding your money, travellers' cheques, and passport. If you feel insecure at any time about your money and valuables, you can always take them into the shower/sea with you.

- It is also a good idea if you are going trekking, as it will keep all the important things dry.

Water purification

There are a few methods of doing this, but you need to ask yourself the question – do I need any of them? If you are going to go trekking, hiking or to any places where the water could be a little dodgy and you won't be close to sources of clean bottled water, then it may be worth taking something.

- Water purification tablets – taste like an old pair of manky pants, but then at least you know that the water is safe. I had some once, never used them, but kept them because I was fascinated by the way they became mouldy... loads of lovely colours! Apparently they work well.
- If you are not going to go off the beaten track, you can buy bottled water just about anywhere now. The European stuff is usually safer than the local variety, but do watch for 'tampering'. If the seal on the top is damaged, or looks as fake as a political manifesto... leave well alone. Or you could buy this stuff, drink it, and then sit on the toilet for the next three days! Your call.

Think light, loose-fitting cotton... as it dries out quickly and is not too hot.

CLOTHES

Hat

- Beware of sun stroke!... when going into the Southern Hemisphere or near the Equator many (like myself) don't realise how hot the sun really is. I'll tell you now... it really does do your head in, making you feel rotten, nauseous, and not at all well... not what you want when everyone else is at the local bar enjoying themselves.
- Also it's necessary to cover up in some countries if entering sacred buildings, etc... especially for the ladies. Usually best to ask. Remember, fashion doesn't matter when you're travelling!

Sarongs

For men and women... no lads, it's not just a skirt! Sarongs are great, and in my eyes essential for backpacking, as they double as sheets, wraps, towels, shawls, beach towel, but are also necessary to wear over your legs when entering sacred buildings in many countries. Cheaper to pick up over there if you can't find one here – you are also more likely to find some funky colours; after all, if you're buying your first sarong... make it a good 'un. David Beckham? Fashion guru? No mate – I've been wearing sarongs for years!!!

Shirt

Light material, plus long sleeved. This stops you being eaten alive by insects and in the event of sunburn will keep you covered up and not irritate the area too much.

Shoes

- Always the big problem. I've always found light trainers to be the best, as when you're walking around a lot in hot countries you'll find 'heavy' trainers sweat profusely and so smell quite badly. If like me you have a problem with cheesy feet... beware! Whatever you do, make sure you break them in well before you go and that you air your shoes as much as possible when you are out there. The odd wash now and again won't go amiss either. If you're not sure, go into a shoe shop and ask their advice about what's best. I normally don't wear socks in hot countries – saves on washing but does mean the shoes will be minging quicker.

- Be aware that you might wear them while walking in the sea or in wet 'jungly' conditions (or something like that). The point here is that if your trainers have that **leather stuff on top**... you're buggered! If you've had them before, you know how after a fair bit of 'wear and tear' the leather rots/breaks up. Well, wearing them the whole time will lead to them disintegrating very quickly. **'Synthetic' is the name of the game here.** If you're trying to be fashionable – forget it. Think practical, as no one really cares and you need footwear that is going to last.

- Desert Boots are great for travelling. Best described as a light but robust low-backed boot, they are comfortable, strong and perfect for general use.

- A lot of people end up wearing thongs (or 'flip flops' as we say in the UK!), which no longer have an untrendy image when you travel, as they really are the most practical things to wear! They're great for temples, hot places, showers (to avoid verrucas), going to the beach, etc. Surf shops (in most high streets now) normally stock a good range – get some tough swimming shorts/gear when you are there at the same time.

Shorts/Skirts

- If in hot countries you'll be in them all the time, so get a few pairs of a tough material.

- Lads can get away very well with swimming shorts if you're going to spend a bit of time on beaches, swimming, etc. Make sure they have a good tough lining, dark one-tone colours are best if you want to head into town with them on and just a T-shirt – tight Speedo's may not help you get into a bar or certain tourist attractions.

- And for the girls, the short wrap around skirt/sarong is ideal for covering a swimming cossie, or just for everyday wear in hot countries.

Smart clothes

You may like to carry a set of 'smart clothes' with you for possible job inteviews, working in, or for going out to smart places. I usually take a smart pair of low-cut shoes (i.e. not ankle high) that can be shined up, a good pair of trousers, a good shirt, and a tie. Girls, a nice set of what is best described as 'black and whites' should also do the job. All these can be used for other purposes and are invaluable (so you'll be glad that you took them) when you need them.

Thermals

If going to cold countries, or even hot countries that may be very cold at night, thermals are great... don't be shy, be warm. So take those Long Johns and wear them with pride! On the odd really cold day when I was a student in Manchester I used to wear them (leftovers from the trip to Russia)... lovely and warm... didn't tell anyone though, until now that is. DOH!

T-shirts/light tops

A few are a good idea, as you will find yourself always wearing and washing these.

- In hot countries you will obviously sweat more, so if you take old ones away with you you might find them falling apart fairly soon, so try to take ones with strong stitching on the shoulders, for example.
- T-shirts with prints on them can be very useful to take as they are good for 'conversation starters'. Wearing a bungee-jumping T-shirt, or one with something about England, windsurfing or football, has led to people coming up to me and starting a conversation. If you have something with your home town/school/university on, you will soon meet people and find out what a small world it is after all!

Trousers/jeans

- Beware if taking jeans: if it's hot, they can be too hot... if they get wet, they'll take ages to dry and can make you very cold... if trekking don't wear them because if they do get wet, they can lead to hypothermia. They are bulky, but are handy to go out at night.
- Light material trousers are best, as they are cool and not too bulky to pack.

Underwear

As much as you think necessary but, again, it's easy to wash and quick to dry so don't go overboard. It fills up the gaps in your backpack nicely, but will be a pain if it doesn't get used. Be wary about 'going commando' in countries with little bastard bugs with pincers and a nasty bite. Your 'bits' make a nice target and, trust me, it hurts!

Warm sweatshirt
Of some kind... heavy + bulky, so keep to bare minimum.

If one of your first stopping off points is a country like America or Asia where clothes are a lot cheaper than over here, why not save some money and wait until you get there to buy your clothes? However, if you are a terrible shopper, and the sight of all those cheap clothes would make you flip out, and spend, spend, spend... then buy at home – some backpackers have been known to spend most of their money at their first stop, fill their packs with unwanted junk and suffer for the rest of the trip.

➤ NB: You may well experience weight change... even Tony lost some weight, although you wouldn't think it to see him now. So do think about loose-fitting clothes. They'll not only be more comfortable for when you are travelling around, but also more practical, as with drawstring/elastic at the top, they'll always be OK if the pounds come on/off. Fashion? Remember that it doesn't count when you travel, so be practical.

OTHER POSSIBLE ITEMS

Balloons/pens
You'll meet a lot of 'fascinated' kids on the way; it's always nice to give them little presents like these that they'll really like.

Books
Heavy/bulky to carry, but easy to swap with other backpackers. In a lot of hostels you will find a book-swapping shelf where you can swap your books for free.

Map of the world
Always good to have one, so at least you know generally where you are and where you're going. Good as a visual aid when getting tips on places.

Apparently you can 'borrow' them from the airline magazines, but again I wouldn't know anything about this terrible practice. On the other hand, the magazines are just thrown away when they are out of date, so why not put parts of it to good use?

Marmite
It is good for you, lasts for ages and makes a great snack with a loaf of bread (just make sure it is stored in an unbreakable place, or you'll have that lovely Marmitey smell following you everywhere!).

Photos of family
So you know why you left home for eight months! Also makes you a 'real' person (i.e. not just a 'travel bum') if you have problems with officials.

> **PACKING?... THE RULES ARE SIMPLE:**

If you can't afford to lose it
If you don't think you need it
If you can buy it cheaper overseas
If it's bigger than your backpack
If it weighs more than you

DON'T TAKE IT

Chapter 4

Parents

6 *Travel, in the younger sort, is part of education:
in the elder, a part of experience* 9

Francis Bacon

Remember: Mums worry!

When talking (often... too often maybe!) about writing this book, the subject of parents always invariably arose. As I bore people to sleep with tales of scuba diving on the Great Barrier Reef, sky diving in Canada, the beaches of Thailand, and the arrogance of Americans (not all, just a few!), many parents ask 'Would you send your own son/daughter off round the world?' To this I have no real answer, as at 22 the thought of having children sounds as appetising as a naked roll in the snow with Gordon Brown! I would of course say '**YES!**', as the education, experience and maturity that they will gain will be invaluable in life. When the time comes that I will buy a pair of slippers and a pipe, settle down, have kids, allow them to grow up, and then approach the age of 18, I will actively encourage them to travel and broaden their horizons.

The problems of letting go

Many parents remark that their children certainly do change when they travel, many 'for the better' (as in the poem in the front of my book). But it is easy to forget that at the age of 18+ we are in fact adults. Of course, everyone is different. Some families actively encourage their children to move away, 'grow up', and find their feet in life. Others, however, find it difficult to let go, staying very protective, maybe not being able to come to terms with the fact that their children have grown up. I'm not sure if it is a feeling of all those years put into a child's life, the shaping, the expense, the good and the bad times, or just the feeling of being in control and not wanting to lose that control. At the end of the day, you are your parents' children and it is often difficult for them to let you go off and do something which they may see as dangerous. This is especially true since the Childers Hostel fire, September 11th, the Bali bomb and the highly publicised deaths of a few young backpackers over the past couple of years. Of course they are going to worry and the current uncertain global climate is quite simply going to make them 'kak it' even more. It's your job, therefore, to make them see that it isn't as dangerous as they think and that you're doing it for your own good.

Everyone is so different in what they believe in, and what they do. This is what I find very interesting, and yet very difficult about this subject. For instance, I know that a lot of parents will read this section of the book. Although they like to sit back and watch what you do from a distance, the interest is always there. The conclusion I have drawn from the contributors to this book is that parents seem to lie in two camps. Either they are keen to get involved, with many contributors catching their parents sneakily reading up on places, reading the Lonely Planet guides and trying to help out as much as possible... or they have seen a total disinterest until just before take-off, or until you actually return.

Parents will worry, because it is their job to worry!

I realised at the start that this section is going to be an absolute nightmare to write, but I think that it is one of the most important chapters in the book. There are always a lot of things that we always want to say to each other, but which never come out. There are a lot of things that your parents would like you to know, but won't say... like the fact that they do care a helluva lot about you, and that if you don't get in contact for a couple of months they **will** worry about you! You may think that when you go out at night and say that you will be back very late that they won't particularly care. However, many won't sleep easy until they know that you are safely home. So your decision to go off travelling around the world won't simply be taken with a pinch of salt!

So what do I hope to achieve in this chapter?

Well, just to bring up a few issues really.

- I feel that good communication on the subject is always best before you go.
- Once you've gone, they want to know what you are up to.
- They would also like to know roughly where you are.
- Finally, they would like to have a rough idea of what your plans are.

Apparently there is nothing worse than your parents answering questions from friends and family about you while you are away starting with the words 'I really don't know... ', 'He/She never told me... ' or, 'Well I haven't heard for a while, but I'm assuming that he/she is all right!' So get the communicating part right from the start after you have made the decision to go.

Learn from my mistakes!

For me this is a very personal wish. I had opposition from my dad all the way. His refusal to accept that I was finally reaching adulthood turned my gapyear before university into a real struggle. It made me resent him, and made it very difficult to sort myself out before I left. By the time I left, I couldn't wait to get away. This is how it **shouldn't be**, and so I hope that I am in a great position to make sure others learn from my mistakes.

Looking back on it now, **persevering and fighting for my dream of going travelling around the world was the best move I ever made**. Why? Because my dad thought that he knew what was best for me. He wouldn't accept that possibly I knew what I wanted to do and that I was in charge of my own life. Unfortunately there is an acceptance in this world that everyone should do what is socially acceptable, and what is the norm. In our family, everyone has gone to school, got their exams, got into university, and got jobs. Work, work, work, and then die. Doesn't that sound morbid! But true. It always seems to me that there is this unwritten law which says that you should do this, and any break from this is frowned upon. Well frown upon me then! I did it, and I'm glad that I did it!

I think it is more to do with the fact that the people who are frowning upon you are those ones who haven't done all that they would have liked with their lives, and who are jealous of you for breaking from the norm and doing something exciting. Many parents who haven't travelled may see it as nothing more than a glorified holiday, and will refuse to see any benefits that you could get from it at all. Those that have, like Tony's dad (who was in the merchant navy), believe that their children should see the world as they did.

➤ But at the end of the day it's what you get out of it that counts...

Grab hold of your own life!

I suffer constant jibes from my parents along the lines, 'Isn't it about time you got a job?' Why? I don't feel that I'm ready just yet to jump on the long 43-year slog to my retirement! Yes, I will get down to getting a job soon.

We're now growing up in a society where people have 'portfolio careers', where we change jobs every three to five years. There is no such thing as a 'career for life' anymore, so why be forced into one? If you don't know what you want to do with your life – fine! Take your time. You're not a sheep are you? So don't follow others around!

Many will say that you are wasting a year in life

Rubbish, you are gaining a year of incredible worldly experiences. The difference between working 43 years and 44 years! Ridiculous eh? Don't let your parents hold you back because they haven't been able to do what you are doing (they forget that it was actually different in their day), or because they think it is about time that you went to college/got a job. If you have to struggle for it, then good luck, I know how difficult it is going to be for you. But if it can be any other way, then do it. Don't end up resenting your parents, as they are only looking out for your best interests.

➤ **That's the ironic thing, the reason so many of us fall out with our parents at this time is that we are both struggling to look after our own interests!**

The only answer is 'Well, who rules your life then?' I'm sure that if you show them that you want to be in control of your own life, and do what you want to do... in a sane manner of course!... then they will be proud of you, and give you all the help possible. Try and make them see it from your point of view. They will eventually become resigned to the fact that you are off and so come round in the end. Remember, they probably won't want to alienate you, just as much as you don't want to alienate them.

Reassurance

All they want, need and, to be honest, deserve to get is a bit of reassurance:

- that you will be all right
- that you will be sensible at all times
- and that you'll ring/write home regularly. *This is especially important if you are aware that something has happened near to where you are – e.g. thousands of parents spent a miserable few days worried that their children had been killed in the Bali bomb, when in fact they were safely miles away oblivious to it all. Whatever happens promise your parents that you will keep in touch and for God's sake make sure that you do…*
- and at times of need – don't be proud!

Forgive the sterotypes, but from my experience your parents will provide two different reactions:

- **Mums will tend to worry about 'mumish' things**, i.e. will you eat properly, get a horrible disease, mugged, etc.
- **Dads tend to worry about the financial side**, i.e. organising your finances, being left with large credit card bills/letters blackmailing him for more money… combined with your mum nagging him about leaving you to starve on the other side of the world!
- **Dads will also worry about mumish things, but after years of leaving it up to your mum, will continue to do so here!**

This is all unavoidable, but quite nice in a way, because you realise that despite everything you thought in your teen years, they are not out to get you and that they really do care!

Support and advice from your planning stages right up to your leaving will always be appreciated, and is the best start to your trip. If they want to get involved, let them! Who else will persuade those distant relatives to give you

Can you cook? Why not get a crash course off your mum or dad? It's something that you can practise every day before you leave. It will further reassure your parents that you will in fact feed yourself while you're away. It is also a lot cheaper, and better for you, than that 'Wopper McDogburger' at the local take-away!

useful presents for your travels for Christmas? Who else will remind you about your doctor's appointments, or give you valuable tips about packing?

Never, on any account, go off round the world without letting your parents know. 'Yeah, hi mum, no I'm not at Jason's, I'm in Bangkok. What do you mean "when am I coming home?" I don't know, in a year or so, a bit longer maybe? Sorry... what exactly do you mean about Dad setting fire to my bedroom...!' It won't be appreciated!

Keep your parents informed

- When you have made that decision to travel and actually have a route booked and sorted out, keep your parents 'in the know'.
- Give them a general outline of what the route is and make them aware (and of course be aware yourself!) that the route might actually change.
- And if you find that the route does change for whatever circumstances, say that you will inform them... and make sure you do; they'll thank you for it!

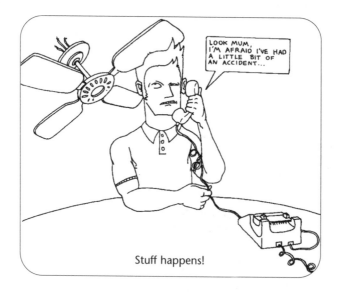

Stuff happens!

There have been a couple of times when I have literally gone walkabout and my parents didn't really know where I was. I didn't really care at the time because I was having a great laugh and so didn't really think about anybody else. In fact there was a time on my first trip when I didn't speak to my parents for a fair while, and then I rang up (feeling a bit low and sorry for myself) having just had a ceiling fan extracted from my head! All I wanted was a bit of sympathy... but looking back on it now it wasn't the best thing I'd ever done, not getting in touch for a while and then ringing up because I had damaged myself. I guess they started to believe that I would only ring if I was in trouble or something.

This was a habit I got out of pretty damn quick after I got a major telling-off from a 'mother' that I met while diving on the Barrier Reef up in Cairns. I reckon this woman went round making backpackers feel guilty for a living. However... the message got across and it hit home hard.

KEEPING IN TOUCH

Bingo! Think I've hit the big one here! From what I've just said above, you'll probably gather how important I think keeping in touch with your family is when you travel, so **sort this one out between yourselves before you go and you'll all be a lot happier**. There are a few alternatives to choose from, so think about them all and come to a few firm decisions before leaving about how you are going to keep in touch and roughly when, rather than getting on the plane throwing a few half-hearted promises around. By the time you wave goodbye at the airport, your parents need to be comfortable and happy about when they are going to hear from you again!

Your parents don't want to know that when you get bored one day, and have nothing else to do, that you'll send them a scatty postcard, indicating nothing more than the rough area of the world that you are in, the fact that at the time of writing you obviously had some sort of health (and a limb to write with), and that you couldn't care less if they hear from you at all. What

BIG TIP TIME

As with any of the methods I am about to talk about, please don't make it a 'regular' thing. By all means make it regular in the sense that you will ring/write every once in a while... to be agreed by you. But not every Sunday, or the first Monday of the month at 6pm, or anything like that. Why not? Well because your parents will have it written down on the calendar, and may well look forward to the call with a big list of things to tell you, news, friends, etc. Each call will be built up, by telling friends/relatives that they are to hear from you on that day, and that they will in turn recount your news in the days following.

Meanwhile... At 6pm, on the first Monday of the month you are island hopping in Indonesia. At the precise moment that your mum is waiting for that call, you are at a beach party. In front of you are a lot of very happy people, loads of new friends, maybe a bit of a hunk/babe that you are eyeing up (and the more alcohol you have, the tastier they look!... been there eh!!), a lot of cheap beer, and not a telephone in sight. As for remembering that time on that day in that month... you lost track of time eight days ago when you all decided to hide your watches away, and live by the day, and not by the time. IT HAPPENS!!

So, your mum doesn't get the call, panics a bit, but calms down thinking there must be another explanation. The phone rings. She snaps it up... it's your gran, wondering how you are. Your mum says that you failed to call. Gran starts to reassure your mum, but brings the subject up of the dangers of travel (false of course). Your mum

TOP TIP!
TOM'S
TOP TIP!

panics again. All through the week she doesn't sleep as everyone she meets asks her about you, and she says that she is still waiting to hear. They all reassure her, but always seem to add to her worry.

One week later: you get back to the mainland, stay in a hostel, and realise that you are a week late. Ah well, I'm a week late already... so you leave it a couple of days! Finally you ring. You are calmly asked why you didn't ring, but you are so thrilled at what you have just done that thoughts of your parents' worry go right over your head. After the call, you go off to the beach/pub, pleased at catching up on news from home, oblivious of the worry. Your mum sits there, relieved, but drained by the worry.

And so here we have it... a page in the life of a 'regular phonecaller' who fails to call. I'm as guilty as the next person for not keeping in touch properly, but I hope at least that my parents knew that I would be in touch some time. Your parents will always think the worst, unless you make sure that they know exactly what is going on. Events like this above, which as I'm sure you'll realise are very common, are unnecessary and avoidable. Just as long as you realise that your parents will worry, and that it is your 'duty' to keep them informed, you should spare them this. Nuff said!

they want to hear is that you will write from every country, so that they can map your progress, or ring on 'Days' that you can't possibly forget, such as your birthday, Cup Final day, etc.! It's not only for their benefit, it might be for you as well. What if they need to get in touch with you for some important reason? Something you would like to know? This pact, and trust that you will actually keep in touch, really does help a lot. Please treat this keeping in touch thing seriously.

Email

For those of you who don't know what I am talking about – put down the encyclopedia, head to the front door and open it. You will notice that there is a world out there that has changed since you last looked! For those of you who have parents who don't know what this word means, or have actually understood it but are reluctant to let 'it' in the house... time to sort out a plan!

Hopefully you know how to use the Internet, email and all that jazz. If you don't, I would suggest you ask someone who knows to show you how to do it as soon as possible, rather than me trying to give you an on-the-spot tutorial that will probably be wrong...

1. Get a free email account like a Hotmail account. Hotmail is good because the majority of travellers use it and it is recognised around the world. Unfortunately, you also get a lot of unwanted spam/junk mail and it is very difficult to get a decent address which is easy to remember, explain and looks OK. Have a look around at other options – Yahoo and Talk 21 are great free email alternatives.

2. If your parents don't have email set up properly – sort their system out and get them used to it. If they don't have the Internet, find a friend of theirs/neighbour who does and sort out a system whereby they can receive emails on your parents' behalf – print them out, stick them in an envelope and post them through the door.

3. Set up your address list properly, get email addresses for everyone you want to keep in touch with and think about using the options available to stick in birthdays, addresses and stuff you really should remember even though you have the excuse of being thousands of miles away. Saves you the time and expense of doing this from an Internet café in the Back of Beyond.

4. Send yourself emails of your important details such as reference numbers, travellers' cheque numbers, passport numbers etc., and also anything else that might be useful to you while you are away. Ultimately you should think about using your email account as your floating safe deposit box – everything important should be in there so you can access it while on your travels. Attach your CV, scanned references and anything that can be printed off and used to help you find work or prove who you are.

Have a search of the web and find a pile of sites which could be useful to you while travelling. Also, find sites which could be useful to your parents while you are away. Copy and paste the links into an email and send them to yourself and your parents so you can simply head to that email, click on the link and you'll be there.

It's great to get emails while you're travelling, but ask people to be as brief as possible, as some places are extremely expensive to pick up your mail – especially in any place which turns out to be a converted cow shed with the owner's son pedalling like mad in the corner to keep the generator going as his wife attempts to sell you luke-warm coke (and you think I'm joking right?). Massive files may take forever to download or may be impossible to open. All worth thinking about.

Post Restante

For those who prefer to get physical post or who are not too happy using the Internet, there is another way of keeping in touch.

Post what???? Well this is a system that works extremely well, and one which is very under-used for what it is. 'Post Restante' is simply the name of a postal system in which letters that are sent to you stay in the post office that they have been sent to and wait for you to pick them up (with the use of identification). If you don't pick them up within their alloted time, which can be anything up to six months, they will be sent back 'return to sender'. Goodness knows why it is called Post Restante, daft if you ask me!

How does it work?

Example:
I know that my daughter Claire Sedding will be in Sydney in April:

I therefore address the envelope as follows...

```
AIR MAIL        ■ ■ ■

Miss Claire Sedding
Post Restante,
GPO,
Sydney,
AUSTRALIA.
```

This letter, when it reaches Sydney, will stay there for up to a month, and if not collected it will be sent back 'Return to sender' – so remember to put your address on the back of the envelope. In the GPOs they may well publish a list of all the mail which is in, or have a box where it is filed alphabetically for you to sort through. All you need then is your passport or some form of ID to pick your post up. The only problem is, for example, with names like mine. Some people call me Thomas Griffiths, others Tom Griffiths (preferred... just to let you know!), some may put T. Griffiths, others T.P. Griffiths, finally, some may put Griffiths Tom/Thomas. These will all be filed under their different alphabetical areas, so it is always worth asking people to address with the same title, or you'll end up looking under all possibilities. This is especially true in countries with a different language and alphabet. Definitely not worth friends using your nickname, unless you are expecting it of course.

Basically, wherever you go in the world (just about), if your family or friends write to the main post office (GPO) in whatever town you are staying in, the letter should be held in that post office in the Post Restante area. This depends on whether the town is on the backpacker trail. Obviously, it is better to use capital cities or major towns as collecting points for your mail, as you have more guarantee that you will receive it.

➤ NB: When going to collect your mail make sure that you go to the correct post office, as I got caught out on this one. Ask at the post office if they have the main/only Post Restante system in the town and, if not, find out where you should go.

Receiving letters

We all like to receive letters, in fact there is nothing better than going to the post office, having been away from home for a bit, to find a letter or a parcel waiting for you. Simple news from home, or just general chat about things and people that you haven't heard from or seen for a while is one of the best things in the world. So do make sure you sort out a few plans before you shoot off, letting people (including your family) know roughly where you'll be and at what time... and get your mates to keep sending those letters, snippets of news and general bits of rubbish that they know will make you smile!

Keep in touch with travelling friends

This system is also useful for seeing if any of your friends are in town if there is a list published on the wall, or if you have access to the mail. However, refrain from writing messages on the letters that may be funny to you and your mate, but appear obscene to their parents. Why I say this is that I happened to stumble across a letter for my friend in Ko Samui, Thailand. So I grabbed a pen and wrote my address on the island on the envelope, as well as a message which I thought was hilarious at the time. Unknown to me... Ben had already left Ko Samui, and had not picked up his mum's letter. Did I hear anyone say Return to Sender? So my hilarious messages... winged their way like a little white dove... back to his mum. Good one Tom! Right comedian you turned out to be!

Post Restante is also very useful for keeping in touch with other backpackers who are also on the move in areas where Internet access is poor. If you tell friends to expect a letter in Bali, for example, even if you arrive a week earlier/later than each other, you will know where they are. If you move on, you can leave a chain of messages at the post offices en route, so they can catch you up somewhere. This system isn't very well publicised, but it does work, so use it. Obviously email is quicker and easier, but in areas where there is no access to the Internet, this still works fine.

American Express travellers' cheques

I've put this in the Post Restante section because if you have AMEX travellers' cheques they basically offer the same system. They run a postal service where they will hold post for three months for you. You will get a list of their addresses, and they are very reliable. Your parents are also able to trace where you are and where you have been as they keep a record of where you have cashed your cheques on file.

Voice-mail services

Voice-mail is another option you may want to think about, as it is always nice for people to hear your voice and for you to hear theirs. Voice-mail is one of these things which has become a little unfashionable with the rise of the mobile phone and the Internet, which means that it is cheap now! BT now offer 'call minder' free and there are other free services similar to this which are basic answerphones which you can operate remotely. If you can operate it remotely, i.e. ring it from anywhere in the world to pick up messages and change your greeting, it can be quite a useful communication tool.

➤ **For example**... '*Hi there, it's now May 8th and I landed in Sydney two days ago. I'm fine and having a fantastic time. I'll be staying at the xxxxxxxxx hostel for a week and then moving on to Byron Bay. If you want to get in touch my number is xxxxxxxxx and I'm in room 21. If you want to write to me, write to the Post Restante in Brisbane, as I'll be there around the beginning of June. Just to remind you, my email is xxxxx@xxxxxx.com. Mum you'd love it out here, the beaches are full of hunky Aussie lifeguards... wish you were here? The suntan's coming on well, but then you probably don't want to hear that... well tough! Leave a short message as it's expensive to pick them up, but I'd love to hear from you.*'

As you travel around you can leave your number with people and change the messages so that everyone can keep track of how you are getting on. My only advice would be to tell people not to leave long messages, otherwise voice-mail becomes too expensive to use and so useless. Use it in conjunction with a calling card of some description and it gives you another effective way of keeping in touch.

Why is it a good idea?

- It is always nice to hear your friend's voices as you travel around... news, gossip, etc.
- Family and friends can always check on the progress of your travels.
- It can cost you as little as the price of a stamp to keep in touch.
- You can use it as a way of meeting up with other travellers... 'I'll be in xxxxx on the 24th...'
- There are no postal delays or worries about time differences.

Foreign relatives/long-distance friends

There is often a big temptation to use foreign relatives as postal/contact points. Beware, sometimes your parents think it's a good idea for you to visit these people as they don't see much of them. Have you ever met them? Are you just being used as a family 'pawn' to relieve some guilt? Don't get me wrong, it is extremely nice to receive some home comforts when you have been without them for a while. However, it can also be extremely awkward, especially if you don't know them too well, as you may feel that you are imposing.

➤ **If you would like to see them, then it is a very good idea to use them as a postal/contact point.**

- If not too keen, beware. They may well live 'out in the sticks' somewhere, which may mean splitting up from a group of friends to trek off to them to pick up some post.
- You might feel this to be unnecessary and cumbersome at the time, especially if you're forced to play 'catch up' with your mates (although very easy to do).
- So, before you go, do check to find if the relative really is 'By a bridge, Up a creek, Timbuctoo', or near to the well-beaten backpacker trail.

At this point I can hear a few 'travellers' groaning... of course if they do live out in the sticks, it may well be the perfect opportunity for you to see a real bit of the country. An old family friend of ours (who I'd never met) lived in the hills behind Surfers Paradise in Australia. Aged 50, she had reappeared on the scene on a Harley Davidson motorbike, having had no real family contact for years. We thought we'd go have a look see! Best decision we ever made. A real experience and saw some fantastic parts of Australia that we would otherwise have missed.

Postcards

Who hasn't heard the phrase 'Send us a postcard!' It is always said, yet always laughed off as a joke. But, as you will see from what I have said before, it is definitely worth doing as it will save parents a lot of anxiety. But again, on the regularity issue, beware! If your parents are used to them coming at regular intervals, when one doesn't arrive they may worry. Postcards easily get lost as they are not seen as priority mail.

This can be avoided by putting them into envelopes – loses the attraction of them, but at least you know that they'll arrive. I laughed at Tony for having a load of self-addressed envelopes in his pack to put postcards in. However, a few months down the line when a load of mine hadn't arrived, it suddenly looked like a good idea! Possibly a good idea for you? However, note that this method can be a bit more expensive as it is treated like a letter and is also heavier with the envelope.

Your parents may also be more receptive to helping you out when you return (i.e. with requests for cash) if they know that you made an effort to remember them while you were away. If you do have a dodgy experience, it is probably best not to tell them before you get home, they'll only worry. I suppose 'What they don't know won't hurt them', just as long as you don't find yourself in a position where you need to talk to them about it. Just be careful about unnecessary worry.

Phone calls

There are phones all over the world now, and in all sorts of isolated places. Just a quick 10 seconds saying where you are, where you're going, and that you're fine and having fun will make a huge difference to mum and dad's worries at home. However, if any of the above are not true, don't ring and try to lie to them, as invariably they will be able to tell if you are lying. This will make things even worse for them. Lots of 10-second phone calls will not cost too much and are a small price to pay for peace of mind. There are a few good communication cards out there. BT chargecards are notoriously expensive, so unless you want Sri Lanka's deficit on your phone bill, think twice about using this method. Pre-paid international calling cards are the best bet – so at least you know where you stand with the cash you are spending.

At home, your parents need to get themselves an account with a company that do cheap international calls – I have one of these and, as mentioned before in Packing, use it to call my brother in Australia for 5p per minute. You need to work out a system with your parents whereby you contact them to give them your phone number either by a reverse charge call, using your pre-paid calling card or, more simply, by emailing them – and then they call you back using the cheap international calls, which are always going to be far cheaper from a landline from home.

Ever thought of taping yourself?

This is something that my family has done for years to keep in touch with Aunty Nicky out in Australia, but I have only just had it mentioned to me recently and I think that it is definitely worth considering. We used to use the small Dictaphone tapes, but it is perfectly possible with a normal cassette. After a few months, why not record yourself onto a cassette (you'll easily find somewhere to do it), and then send that to your family? Better than any postcard or letter, and it really will give them a flavour of what you are up to. Well, worth a mention anyway!

And finally...

A brief message to any parents reading this section: thinking that it might well be alright letting your 'little darlings' leave the nest for the wide blue yonder? I hope so! **It's about time that we fell on our backsides and learnt to pick ourselves up.** We can do it. We will be all right. After all, you've done it, so why shouldn't we?

Well... what are you waiting for?

Chapter 5

Health and emergencies

❝ He who has health has hope,
and he who has hope has everything ❞

Arab Proverb

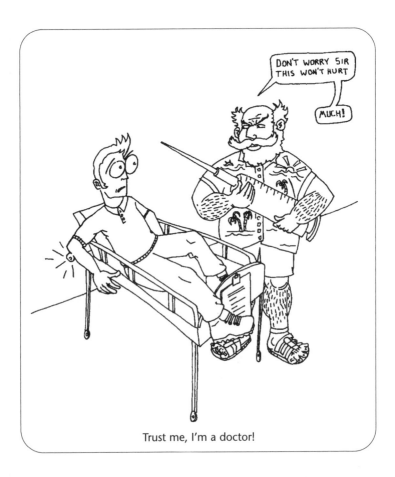

Trust me, I'm a doctor!

For general points on health, see '**Tips, hints and problems**', Health.)

This is a serious issue and needs good discussion before you go

The most important thing you have to look after while you are away is you. Your health must always be of number one importance and should never be ignored. Accidents may, and will, happen – they do in your everyday life – but we all come back safely, maybe just a little more 'misshapen' than before. I can bear testament to that, having got five stitches in my head, after accidentally putting it in a ceiling fan – long story – but I was stone-cold sober at the time! (If ever you go to the Twenty Degrees South Hostel in Airlie Beach, Australia, do look for a dented fan on one of the ceilings in one of the rooms, autographed by yours truly!) I have also had Tropical Ear (an ear infection caused by not drying my ears out properly after going in the sea)... which was very painful, and always cuts and bruises from being a lumbering fool every once in a while – nothing has changed since I used to come home from school with grazed knees and blood spurting from all sorts of limbs and orifices!

General travelling around will keep you fit; for many this is down to the amount of walking, swimming and outdoor activities that you may do. You'll find that it's cheaper (and nicer – so you can see stuff) to walk to the shops/town and back; and having all the time in the world, good weather, etc., you may find that you'll be walking four miles a day and not even noticing! Also the time spent outdoors will do wonders for your respiratory system. However, you need to watch out in polluted cities like Bangkok where the effects of the heat and the pollution quite literally did my head in. However, you're sure to notice the difference a bit of time outside in the good weather does to you, especially the effect of a bit of sun and sand on your skin.

However, it is when you feel that there is possibly something wrong with you that you must watch out for yourself. I'm very guilty of this, often thinking that if I ignore it that the symptoms will go away. What if it doesn't and it gets worse...? You are a long way from home and your local GP. There are countless stories of backpackers who think that they have the symptoms say of a cold, but find that it turns into some local/Southern Hemisphere disease...

- Cerebral malaria feels like sunstroke... nausea, dizziness, etc.
- Giardia starts with stomach cramps, followed by diarrhoea and bloating.
- Amoebic dysentery is bad diarrhoea, sometimes with blood in it.
- Bilharzia, caught from swimming in inland lakes or rivers, results in fever and anaemia.

Now this isn't an excuse for all you hypochondriacs out there to start feeling ill at every possible moment, thinking that malaria is setting in. It probably isn't... all I'm saying is that if you really aren't well, get yourself looked at, and treat yourself properly.

Why not take a first aid course?

It is well worth thinking about taking a first aid course through St Johns Ambulance before you go. It is very useful to have done it and could save you a lot of pain, time and worry if you know how to look after/treat yourself properly. You may well end up saving someone else's life someday, too.

Get the right medical kit and sterilised kit

In the '**Packing**' section of this book there is advice on the type of medi-kit and steri-kit to buy; it is important that you get the right ones to help you look after yourself.

The best bet here is to give you a few thoughts and pointers in the right direction to get you started and hopefully get you to think about a few of the issues you need to be aware of.

The sun

...can be extremely dangerous. Remember, this is no longer your two weeks in Lanzarote with your family or your lads'/lassies' summer in Ayia Napa, where the focus is on getting a tan quickly to impress your mates and add to your pulling potential. Things are very different when you're out on the road where you may be exposed to the sun regularly for long periods of time over the course of a few months. Wearing a hat can help to avoid sunstroke (which is extremely unpleasant), and skin cancer is avoided with good high-factor suncreams (at least SPF 15) and staying out of the strong midday sun. I wouldn't worry about getting a suntan; it will happen whether you like it or not if you are in a hot country... just take your time. Be warned, the sun in Southern Hemisphere or Equatorial countries is surprisingly hot! I don't normally burn, and go brown very quickly due to my olive skin... I started off with Factor 6 in Fiji, and burnt like crazy! Painful – yes. Don't do it... you'll tan just as well with a Factor 15.

Sexually transmitted diseases (STDs)

AIDS and STDs are easily avoided by taking precautions and with safe sex. I'm not going to lie or kid you – there are many backpacker towns where STDs are rife and the number of cases of AIDS among backpackers is alarmingly on the rise. You can catch STDs and you can certainly catch AIDS, BUT only if you don't take the usual precautions. Yup, it terrifies me, too, but then I always know where the boundaries lie and self-preservation is high on my personal agenda. If you're going to do stupid things and take risks – that's your problem, not mine.

Eating and drinking

Get in the habit of washing your hands before you eat and be 'choosy' about what you eat. Eat healthily, but be careful about seafood, water, ice, salad, i.e. what things are washed in, and what you brush your teeth in. These are things that you will quickly learn to look out for, learning from other people's experiences and by watching what they do/don't do.

It'll grow on you and you'll form good habits. The last thing I want for you is to get paranoid and take all precautions necessary… your own natural defences will tend to weed out anything that you really shouldn't do/eat anyway. If you go away with the thought of looking after yourself, then you'll be fine. The odd dose of 'traveller's tummy' (or the 'galloping trots' as it was affectionately known by Tony and I) is a pain, but has never really hurt anyone. We all get it sometime and laugh about it later.

Jabs/needle phobia

If you need jabs, get them done. Head down to your local GP well before your trip and have a chat about where you are going and when. They will have a Travel Health Clinic or will point you in the direction of one where you can get booked in for any injections you need. Hate needles? Guess what – so do I! Even writing about them right now makes my wrists tingle at the very thought of them. To be honest the jabs aren't too bad. Call me a wuss but I looked the other way and it was over in seconds. The jab of the needle I can deal with, but the sight of them I can't! DON'T whatever you do avoid them because you don't like them. Get all your other bits and pieces up to date while you are there, like Tetanus etc.

A couple of things to be aware of

Below are a couple of things you need to be aware of. I don't want you to panic, but on the other hand I don't want you to ignore what are important health issues. Just take in the info and store it at the back of your mind.

Appendicitis

An ache below your belly button which turns into a sharp pain as it moves out to the right. You will start to get a temperature and start to feel rotten generally. If you have appendicitis, your appendix needs to come out as soon as possible. Yes, it can be extremely serious and very occasionally fatal – only because nothing is done about it and the appendix bursts. If you haven't had your appendix out, then you should be aware of the problem, symptoms, and what to do. Make sure you ask your doctor about this one when you go for your check-up and jabs.

Malaria

Malaria can kill. A mate of mine had the horrific task of having to have her boyfriend, who she was travelling with at the time, cremated out in Sumatra after he died of it. They had stopped taking the malaria tablets because they 'thought they would be OK'. There is also a lot of rubbish advice out there from travellers who are well travelled and think they know the score. Clearly they don't and you should take all advice with a pinch of salt and seek proper medical advice on matters as serious as this.

A few thousand people return to the UK with malaria each year; a few cases become fatal. Two of the most common mistakes are not starting the tablets early enough and finishing too soon. This is why not only should you start taking your tablets a week before you enter an area with malaria (sometimes more – again, get medical advice about the stuff you are taking as sometimes they need to be taken two to three weeks before), but also a month after you leave. There are certain fairly hard mossies and strains of malaria that are becoming resistant to the pills you are going to take, so make sure you get all the up-to-date advice before you head off.

Don't panic!

I don't want you panicking now, having read some of this stuff, just be aware.

Taking medication out with you

- If you are required to take a drug daily, you need to do a bit of planning. A lot will depend on where you go, and what you are planning to do.
- In hot or wet countries you may have difficulty in keeping your medication dry and protected.
- Can you fit it all in your pack, or will you have to get some sent out to you/pick it up from another country?
- You may not be able to send drugs through the post, and on many border crossings you may have problems getting them across.
- If you are in need of some medication in an emergency, will it be available where you are going?
- What if it gets lost/damaged?

Problems like these may lead to an abrupt end to your trip, something you obviously won't want.

Planning and strategies are best thought about now.

➤ **NB: IF YOU HAVE TO CARRY MEDICINE MAKE SURE THAT YOU HAVE A DOCTOR'S NOTE IN CASE YOU ARE STOPPED BY CUSTOMS OR IF YOU NEED TO REPLACE IT.**

SARS

At the time of writing, in late spring of 2003, SARS (Severe Acute Respiratory Syndrome) has been getting a huge amount of very scary press coverage worldwide. The outbreak may be contained but in case it isn't this is what you need to know... The symptoms are very similar to flu – a raging fever, headache, sore throat and coughing. The illness kills (on average) six or seven people out of every hundred infected. Precisely how SARS is transmitted is not yet known, but it is likely that the virus is transmitted by 'close contact', meaning sharing the same living space, being around when a sufferer sneezes or coughs, or anything more intimate than a hug.

It's important to strike a balance between being careful and overreacting. You may well be at risk if you're planning to travel to any part of South-East Asia, and the nature of the virus means that it's hard to actively protect yourself. As at present there is no vaccine; the best prevention is by boosting your body's own immune system, having a balanced diet, and being fit and healthy. **As to whether you should continue with your travel plans, you must check the advice given by both the World Health Organization and the Government – bear in mind that the Government's advice may affect your insurance cover**. It's wise to avoid mass hysteria, but just as important to take sensible precautions.

For up-to-date information on this (and other outbreaks of illness likely to affect your travel plans or insurance cover), check the following websites:
http://www.gapyear.com
http://news.bbc.co.uk (the latest BBC reports)
www.who.int/en (the World Health Organization)
http://www.fco.gov.uk (the Foreign and Commonwealth Office)

Serious problems

If there are any serious problems, always get in touch with the Foreign Office straight away on (020) 7270 1500. If you are required to take any regular medication, something which you may not be able to get in a foreign country, then you may need to have it sent out to you. If this is the case then you may require a special licence to have it sent through the post. For further information on this, ring Action Against Drugs on (020) 7273 2183. If you do this in good time, then you will hopefully be able to sort out the paperwork now, rather than having to wait somewhere while all the paperwork goes through. Having tried a dummy run of this myself as a bit of research for this book, I was passed all over the place, and found that there is probably a lot of bureaucracy to get through.

However, I have been assured that in the event of an emergency the Embassy will be very efficient and treat each case separately... so I don't think that you should worry too much.

GOVERNMENTAL HELP AND THE EMBASSY SYSTEM

What the British Consul CAN do...

- issue emergency passports
- contact relatives or friends to ask them to help you with money/tickets
- advise on how to transfer funds
- in emergency, advance money against a sterling cheque for up to £100 supported by a banker's card valid for the appropriate amount
- as a last resort make a repayable loan for repatriation to the UK (exceptional circumstances)
- help you get in touch with local lawyers, interpreters and doctors
- arrange for next of kin to be informed in event of accidents or a death and advise on procedures
- contact and visit British nationals under arrest or in prison
- make representations on your behalf to the local authorities in certain circumstances.

But a Consul CANNOT...

- intervene in court proceedings
- get you out of prison
- give legal advice or instigate court proceedings on your behalf
- get you better treatment in hospital/prison than is provided for local nationals
- investigate a crime
- pay your hotel, legal, medical, or any other bills
- pay for travel tickets for you except in very special circumstances
- undertake work more properly done by travel representatives, airlines, banks or motoring organisations

HELLO MR EMBASSY MAN. COULD YOU PLEASE PHONE MY DAD AND ASK HIM TO SEND MY LUCKY SLIPPERS!!

Making friends

- obtain accommodation, work or a work permit for you
- formally assist dual nationals in the country of their second nationality.

Consular advice

This is simply what you would naturally do if you encountered any problems abroad...

If you have any problems, especially important ones where you are concerned or need some serious advice, get yourself to the nearest Embassy as soon as possible. It is very unlikely that you will need their assistance but, if you do, ask for it, as that is what they are there for... to look after your interests while you are abroad.

Good preparation before you go

- Get full medical insurance.
- Be aware of the laws and obey them.
- When you land in a country, find the address of your nearest Consul... can be found at the airport information places, at the hostels, in the phone books, etc.
- Check out the Foreign Office 'Know Before You Go' campaign, found at www.fco.gov.uk/knowbeforeyougo

Have fun and enjoy yourself

Insurance

This is such an important issue that many people skim over and ignore it. Please don't. What I am about to say is probably one of the most important things points in this book – so listen up!

YOU NEED TO TAKE INSURANCE. There are no 'ifs' and 'buts' or 'maybes' about this. **YOU MUST NOT LEAVE THE COUNTRY WITHOUT INSURANCE.** Unfortunately over 25 per cent of young travellers leave either uninsured or underinsured. I have ALWAYS been guilty of this and now understand the error of my ways.

How did I buy my insurance?

Travel agent: Have you got any insurance yet?
Tom: Nope... do I need it?
Travel agent: Yes you do.
Tom: OK, I'll have one then!
Travel agent: keeeerrrrrrrrrrrching! (sound of the till taking my money)

... and that was it. I had never bought insurance before, had no idea what it was, why I needed it, what it covered me for (I took one look at the masses of small print, panicked and ignored it) and, to be honest, thought I didn't need it. Now, chances are you could be in the same boat. So, now's the time for me to try and sort you out on this one.

Why must you take it?

If things go wrong, for whatever reason, as you can see from the above, the

Foreign Office will do its best to help you out BUT is not in a position to help you out financially. This is where you or your family come in. So let me give you a few real examples:

- A lad fell off a donkey in Spain and broke his thigh. This cost him £8,000.
- A girl got bitten by a mosquito in Mozambique, got malaria, had to be flown home. Cost? £13,000.
- An air ambulance in South Africa will cost you £18,000.
- Any serious traffic accident, especially in the States, could cost anything up to £100,000 – sometimes more.

Now ask yourself – if I got any of the bills above, assuming I'm not insured – who would pay? You? Your parents? Your mates? The milkman? Think about this for a second. Just by not taking insurance you could severely damage/destroy your parent's financial security and you may even cost them their home. If you have insurance, the insurance company pays, with most policies having medical cover of around £5 million, which will sort you out in ANY situation.

DON'T BE SELFISH

Not taking insurance is not only selfish but irresponsible. It is also not fair on others travellers with you who may have to help out financially in an emergency. I have no idea why it isn't law – similar to not being able to drive a car without insurance – that you can't leave the country unless you are insured. NB: The largest medical claim ever was for £750,000, so £3 million will be more than adequate. Don't be sold on the 'unlimited medical cover' as this is just a sales ploy.

A few additional thoughts on insurance

- If you book with a credit card, you might find yourself insured by the credit card company as well. However, these are only good for extra cover, as they don't give you full cover on everything that you may need... but do check out what you are entitled to.
- Baggage insurance. I don't bother with this any more as I've never lost or had anything stolen. My opinion is that clothes can all be bought again very cheaply. However, if you are carrying an expensive camera, Walkman, pair of pants, then maybe this insurance would be advisable for you. Check the value of the camera they give you.
- Cancellation insurance. You may be offered this initially so that if you have to cancel then you won't lose all your money. Again, this will all depend on your circumstances and peace of mind. Some even provide cover for you if you fail your exams and have to resit.

- If travelling with a companion it may be worthwhile informing them about what type of insurance (particularly medical insurance) you have.

Final tips on buying insurance

1. Don't skimp, i.e. never buy insurance on price alone – those offers you may see in the papers for £30 and a free CD may look attractive but could come back to haunt you. You will only realise why it is so cheap when you come to claim. For that extra £100, say, it will be the difference between someone moving heaven and earth to sort you out... or a bodge job in the back of a shed from a bloke called Miguel!
2. Check out exactly what it covers you for. Look for adventure sports, riding mopeds, getting any costs you incur back into your account while you are overseas. Think about EVERYTHING you may possibly do on your travels, e.g. bungee jumping, skiing (in New Zealand!), riding mopeds, etc., and ensure you get cover for it.
3. Read and understand the small print – it's actually not that bad if you take your time over it. If you have problems get your parents to help you out. Repatriation means getting you/your body home – you definitely need this, as it means that you will be flown home for treatment on a decent flight with a few nurses... sounds awesome to me!!
4. Shop around – there are quite a few insurance companies to have a look at.
5. Ask whoever you buy your insurance from about the process of claiming so that you know exactly what to do. Write it down or get them to print it off for you (it is usually in the policy they give you) – and take a copy of this process with you and give a copy to your parents... so you all know what to do in the unlikely event that you have to make a claim.

Claiming on your insurance

No matter what the event is make sure you get hold of all the evidence, receipts, your own statements from witnesses and their contact details, etc. If there has been some type of accident make sure you get photos of anything that you think will help your claim. Remember that the guys who will be assessing your claim will be miles away and only have your evidence to go on. If there is a police report on the incident, get copies of it. Get everything you possibly can. Hopefully the claim will go through quicker and you should have more success being dealt with quickly.

Still unsure about insurance?

If you have any questions, or if you think that you're not covered properly, ring (020) 7600 3333, and you will get through to the Association of British Insurers who will give you advice and full explanations.

Travelling with diabetes

The thought of travel may be appealing to you, but nerves and worries may well put you off. However, travelling with diabetes is possible, and to give you a few thoughts, ideas and guidelines, Ben (my diabetic travelling specialist) has a few points to make...

'Providing you've done your homework, the diabetic traveller has nothing to worry about...'

- Do make sure that any travelling companions understand generally about diabetes and the difference between being 'hypo' and 'hyper', as you well know the dangers but they won't. They need to know what to do in an emergency, especially if you are drunk!

Be aware of your three main concerns:

1. **Supply**
   - How do you get fresh supplies of insulin halfway up a mountain in the Andes?
   - How do you keep your insulin cool?
   - What supplies do you need for your blood-glucose testing kit?
   - How will your equipment stand up to the job in hand?
   - Can electronics/insulin withstand extreme heat/cold, bright sunlight, water immersing, shock, X-ray, etc.? The answer is often no (check with the care team).

2. **Safety and security**
   - For obvious reasons you don't want others to either steal or use your needles.

3. **General health**
   - What if things go horribly wrong?
   - What if you contract dysentery and can't eat?
   - What if you have to go to hospital?
   - What if you can't find enough carbohydrate and have a hypo in a remote area?

How well you respond to these problems depends on your personality and the amount of time you have to prepare for the literally hundreds of scenarios you might have to face on your travels. If you treat it proactively as part of the adventure, you'll be fine. Get scared or panic, and you'll end up in trouble.

➤ **Know yourself and your equipment and think creatively around any problems you encounter.**

- **Before travelling, consult your GP about using an insulin pen if you don't already.** These are simple, clean, effective, and safe in that it is easy to spot if it has been tampered with… and rugged… Imagine messing around with glass phials of insulin in the middle of the Kalahari! They are easier than phials to get through customs unnoticed. Furthermore, you only need to worry about the needle heads that go with them (packs of 100 at the time of writing cost about £8), so make sure you take a needle clipper with you. Whichever bits you take as optional extras, these bits are the most important.
- It is vital to keep insulin cool. The best way is to take some tough container and store the insulin and needles at the bottom of your backpack (coolest place).
- Keep it with you at all times, don't be tempted to put it in the hostel/hotel fridge.
- Store it overnight in some ice or cold water.
- Kiddies' thermos flasks (non-glass) are very useful; one for wet (insulin pens in cold water), one for dry (needles, etc.).
- Another idea may be to sew storage pockets into the inside of your backpack, making sure that they are well padded.
- Freezer packs are another idea and may be worth taking.
- Only carry the insulin stick that you are using at the time and perhaps one spare; likewise with needle heads (assuming use of the pens).
- If you feel your insulin security to have been breached at any time… play it safe, clip the needle, and chuck it away… it's not worth the risk of any kind of infection.
- **Tip:** if you carry a shoulder-slung pouch with you with all your 'goodies' in, at a push you can put it under your clothes at any moment of 'dodginess'.

➤ Always remember that this stuff keeps you alive!

Supply

As it's only possible to carry two or three months' supply of insulin at a time, why not get a load of your favourite goodies and see whether or not the Foreign Office can help with its transportation to one of the Embassies on your route? If you can arrange for something to be sorted out before you go, whereby you know that as soon as you get down to your last supplies you'll be able to pick up some more on your way, then this will give you and your family peace of mind. I have looked into this, and I've found that each case will be treated specially… so I believe that if you put your case over strongly enough, the Embassies will help you out the best that they can.

> In dire need of any sort, head straight for the nearest British Embassy.

Blood testing kits

The best types have a little door which can keep the rain off, and are rugged enough for taking with you. The versions by Boehringer Mannheim (providing they don't get too wet) are OK. Take an immersion bag to keep these in, and Lowe Alpine does a nice washbag which is convenient for the bits and pieces associated. This can pack into around 250–300g.

General health

It is imperative for any travellers with diabetes to have a health check before you go. Newly diagnosed people with diabetes should probably wait until things have settled down before going anywhere too adventurous... but again it is a question of how well you adapt both mentally and physically.

Enjoying yourself

- Avoid quick carbohydrates at the wrong times.
- Alcohol, although a carbohydrate, reduces blood sugar and so increases the chance of a hypo. The key therefore is to get a good, starchy meal of bread, rice or pasta down your neck before getting hammered.
- Narcotics such as amphetamines and ecstasy are definitely out if you're stupid enough to take them, as they affect your metabolic rate.
- Make sure you have sweets or chocolate handy at all times and you'll be fine.

The above information has been checked and approved by the Diabetes UK.

Advice from Diabetes UK

- Before travelling contact your diabetes care team and GP.
- Have a health check.
- Plan your insulin and test strip supplies.

Things to consider:

- identification
- insurance – one that doesn't rule out pre-existing conditions
- illness – make sure you and your companions know what to do
- what to take – how to store insulin in transit
- travelling through time zones
- the effects of extremes of temperature/altitude/bright sunlight on insulin and equipment
- physical activity – adjusting insulin/food intake to more/less activity

- foot care – examine reguarly, seek early treatment for all foot problems
- food – not always available when needed; carry plenty of carbohydrates
- fluids – diet drinks not always available; alcohol affects your blood sugar – never drink on an empty stomach.

If you have any questions, they are very happy for you to get in touch with them: Diabetes UK, 10 Parkway, London NW1 7AA.
Tel: (020) 7424 1000 Fax: (020) 7424 1001 Email: info@diabetes.org.uk

Do get in touch anyway as they produce a number of travel guides, advice booklets and vital information for many different countries.

I'm not qualified to give answers, so take time to look into health issues properly

I really don't have many answers to any difficulties that you may have in this area. It is such a massive field that I wouldn't be able to do it justice, so I won't even attempt it. However, there are a couple of numbers/addresses at the back of the book that you may like to try. In most developed countries you will find no real problems, as many, like Australia, have a 'tit for tat' system with the UK. You will be covered under their health system, and so will receive good care. However, medical insurance (see page 65) is essential and will need looking into fully to find the right policy for any special requirements, so you don't find yourself uninsured due to any small print.

Illness on return

Beware of contagious bacterial infection. A girlfriend of mine once came back from Pakistan with a magnificent dose of Giardia, and while her mother played the fantastic part of Florence Nightingale, she unfortunately came down with it as well... not a pleasant experience at all, as they were both very ill. From time to time, these contagious diseases may be picked up, so it is always best to be vigilant and in touch with a doctor, as the symptoms are often disguised as other things.

Good preparation **before you go** will leave you ready for anything, and help you deal with any situation that arises. And, when you get back, make sure that the only thing you've brought back with you is a suntan!

Chapter 6

Male solo

'*Step into a new world...*
step out a new man' **Billy Connolly**

Who needs a motorbike?

So you're probably thinking... is this really a good idea?

Will I be isolated? Will I be lonely? Many will tend to say that it really depends on the sort of person that you are, and I tend to agree. As a confident person who has absolutely no qualms about going up to anyone and starting a conversation, travelling solo was an easy option for me. **However, do remember that on my first trip I was accompanied by a friend.** Originally I was up for going alone, but going with a long-time school mate seemed to be a better idea for me at the time. (He nearly dropped out at the last minute... but that's Tony and women for you!) Nevertheless, I have met many people who have left their home country with a shyness that you wouldn't believe, a courageous step for which they always have my full admiration, and have been totally transformed into confident, easy-going people. Mind you, for someone to take a big step like this means that they must have a strong willingness to succeed anyway.

You're all in the same boat!

It is easy to forget that while travelling everyone is in the same boat, and it is in fact extremely easy to introduce yourself to strangers and make friends. In hostels and bars all over the world there is a kind of common language learnt and spoken by all... 'Hi I'm xxxx from xxxxxxxx, mind if I join you? So what's your name, and where are you from?' There are no catchy one-liners that we all learnt as kids and sweat over in clubs and pubs... that is, if you have the courage to even make the first move. In fact, for many it may even be a little odd introducing yourself to someone of the same sex! Suddenly, meeting people takes on a whole new perspective and meaning; it's a skill that I believe will be a great asset to you in life.

When I worked as a barman, many people commented on how well I could hold a decent conversation with a stranger at such a young age, and how it was a useful skill to have. This is not just to do with my own confidence, but more to do with meeting people while travelling, and even more so when I was on my own hitching across Canada. When you get into other people's cars they want to know your whole life story before you get out (I can hear my friends saying '... and I bet you gave it to them Tom... !'). You are forced into a position where you have to learn to converse with people well. From then on, it all comes naturally.

The message is therefore simple... **yes it is very easy to meet people and make friends, and you will make friends everywhere you go**. In fact, if you're the kind of chatterbox like myself then you'll perhaps make too many friends and have trouble keeping up with them all.

The advantage of being solo

The advantage of being on your own, therefore, lies in the fact that **you can come and go as you please**... meet up with whoever you want (and whoever you don't want), and go wherever you want to go without having to consult and discuss it with a partner first. If you meet a nice group of Swedish ladies, who want to whisk you off sailing round some tropical islands for a few days... you go! You'll find that you'll join up with groups of people, travel for a bit, and then meet up with others to travel with later on. Depending on the pace of the travelling of the different groups, you'll always be meeting up with someone or other 'down the road' somewhere. In most countries, travelling is very easy, too easy in fact in places such as the east coast of Australia, South East Asia, etc. Very good friends will be made and kept... you'll be able to meet up in other countries if your paths cross again by keeping in good email contact. And when everything is over you'll have reunion parties to look forward to all over the world with your new 'international' address book.

Travelling is great!

➤ Therefore in answering the questions 'will I be isolated and lonely?'... only if you try really hard to be by yourself. If not... you've got to be joking haven't you?

Of course if you make no effort to introduce yourself to people and become a quiet recluse wherever you go, things may be different. But 99 per cent of the time you will find this impossible as everyone is in the same boat, and so you all get to know each other.

Travelling from place to place

Again this is made easy by the people you will meet. Yes, the guidebooks are extremely useful and worth getting for information on places to go and stay, but you'll find your route determined mainly by other people. They'll have been to places you're about to go to, and vice-versa. Over a few beers you'll swap stories, information, etc. about where it is best to be at that time, what there is to see and do, the best bars/clubs, beaches, etc., etc. You'll probably find your plans changing from day to day... which to me is the beauty and attraction of travelling.

Every day is different, and you really don't know what is going to happen tomorrow. We have all made the common mistake when planning our trips of initially saying that we will be 'here for a week', 'there for two', 'this country for a month' and 'returning home on this or that day'. You're probably doing this right now! Don't worry, this is fine to do as it is vital to make those general plans before you go when sorting out your ticket, **but be prepared for those plans to change... and most importantly let them change**. As you have all the time in the world, you'll find that you'll regret not postponing your departure from Bali so you could stay on for a couple of weeks to visit the Indonesian Islands with your friends. Go with the flow... but do remember to divide your time properly, as you don't want to be left with only a week on your ticket, £5 to your name, and the whole of South East Asia to cover!

My friend Tim is testament to travel changes. Having graduated from Sheffield University with a good degree, he worked in England over the summer and then left on a round-the-world trip, intending, as he thought, to be back in June. The following March, he was having an absolute ball out there in Australia and, as far as I can see, had no real reason to come back for a while. Jealous? Of course I was! Six months can easily change to 9 or 12. You are only really constrained if you have to come back for college... some don't, but I really wouldn't advise this.

➤ If you've worked hard enough to get into college, why throw it all away??

Time to slow your life down

If you've just graduated, then the world really is 'your oyster'. As long as the finances hold many end up travelling for three, four, five, or even six years! It is inevitable that you will get the 'Travel Bug'... and not the one that parks you on the toilet for two weeks (although a quick dose of that might come your way if you're lucky – remember that Imodium/industrial cork in your first aid kit!). When the bug hits you'll want to travel on and on. Your home country will seem so far away and unimportant that you'll find you'll enter a kind of relaxed state of mind as you leave the 'rat race' far behind.

'The Fijian Experience'

The experience of leaving the rat race behind that I'm talking about first happened to me in Fiji. For the past four years I had worked very hard for every exam that I took, right the way through GCSEs and 'A' levels. I spent the time after my 'A' levels working at McDonald's, every shift and hour possible. The whole lot was just hectic hectic hectic! The first stop on our world tour was Los Angeles, a city, and a very fast-moving city at that. After that it was Hawaii, again 'stress city' a high level of Americanism and Japanese tourism there. To tell you the truth, we couldn't get out of these two places quick enough. So, still in a kind of 'hurry, rush, speed' kind of a mood, we landed in Fiji. And then? Everything stopped!

In Fiji they have this remarkable thing called 'Fiji time', and it is absolutely fantastic! If the bus driver bothers to get up in the morning… then there will be a bus! If not, then you might have to wait a couple of hours for him to turn up. The true Fijians are incredibly friendly, but sincere with it, and just laugh at all the tourists trying to rush around the islands. I guess you find exactly the same in areas like the Caribbean, and to some extent right on our doorstep in the Republic of Ireland. This relaxed atmosphere forces you to relax… and you do! **I think Tony and I fully realised at that point that it was possibly the first time that we had ever properly relaxed**, and I mean *really slowed down*. You always hear people saying about how relaxed they think they are and how they don't live their life by a routine. But if you ask them what they'll be doing at 11 o'clock on Wednesday morning, or 6.30pm on Friday night… you'll usually get an answer.

➤ Your life is 'ordered' and your own little world is revolving around you without you realising it.

Is this what they call culture shock?

The state of mind that I'm talking about which we experienced in Fiji, and so for the rest of our trip, is one in which you really don't know what is going to happen that afternoon, let alone next Friday night. It's a weird, but extremely nice, feeling… it's almost as if you're experiencing the so-called 'rat race' in every country you visit, **but as a spectator**, sitting at the side and watching everything go by. You'll start to notice the difference between the countries, and between the different people who live side by side within these countries. But more importantly you'll start to notice differences between your country and theirs, and maybe even start to appreciate your own country more, and the differences that exist throughout the world. I guess this is what they call culture, and the realisation that you are undergoing one of those infamous 'culture shocks'! I'm not one of those 'yeah right-on man' travellers, I just appreciate what is around me, and the difference between people and their environments.

You'll always hear people talking knowledgeably about the poverty out in Africa and Asia, for example. **But as far as I'm concerned you won't really appreciate it until you witness it.** For example, we were in a water taxi in Bangkok, a fast little speed boat that flies around the rivers of the city, and we were worried about being splashed by the tiny drops of stinking milky white water that lie stagnating in the river. However, as we moved on, we noticed that the people who live in the shanty towns at the side of the river use it to wash in, for toiletry purposes, and even to wash their food in! Yes I know it is a way of life that they are used to, but to think that we didn't even want to be splashed by this water!?!... A reflection of our culture and just how lucky we really are.

Having relatively nothing with you, and living off as cheap a budget as you can... yet still living like a King/Queen in some of the poorer countries, really makes you appreciate where you come from and your well-off position in this world. It also trivialises a lot of things and makes you realise that to be happy you don't need piles of money and loads of materialistic things, you just need to do what you enjoy in life, and to appreciate the world around you. This is the best thing about talking to people who have come back from their gapyear – we all seem to have this understanding that life is not just about music, pubs and clubs. You really can tell the difference between someone who has taken a gapyear at Fresher's Week and someone who hasn't. Even after university and in the world of work, I think this is still the same. You can't beat life experiences and, unless you've had them, you can never understand them.

So what am I trying to get at here?

This is where I feel my 'real' education is from, learning to understand people and what they believe in... which is made even easier by travelling solo, as you have no other influences on your thoughts. I also believe it makes you more aware of yourself, who you are, and what role you play in society. As for myself, I've really learnt how lucky I am in relation to others in this world. This is something you can't change. But the important thing is that you are aware of the fact, which I believe makes you a broader and better person, as you escape the narrowness of just thinking about yourself and your own little world. That is my belief; others may, and do, think differently. All I am trying to say is that by the time you return you will be a different/better person... which is a nice thought, eh?

My personal experience of travelling solo

Yes it can be lonely on the very odd occasion, and although you are going to meet loads of other travellers you may well get stuck with a few that you don't find the easiest to get on with. However, in our experience, because you do have this freedom to do exactly what you want, you can easily avoid these ones and hook up with friends that you do instantly click with, and have a laugh. An added advantage of travelling solo is that you get to meet more local people and you'll often get invited into, and become part of, a community somewhere. You'll be the 'new boy' in town, be a bit of a star, a known person, and receive all the hospitality that you can cope with. It's an experience that you'll never forget... warmth and friendliness from total strangers. You'll be 'mothered' and looked after, treated to this and treated to that.

There's an expression: 'What goes around comes around.' When I was in Canada, I had very little money and I lived off the kindness of people. I never begged, hinted, or made people feel guilty. My plan was to go as far as I could on the money that I had, and simply return home when the pot ran dry. However, I didn't need to, as I met kindness practically everywhere I went.

➤ **By being agreeable, polite and, as far as I saw it, a good representative of my country... I was literally offered the earth.**

I had strangers sharing camping slots with me, buying me dinner/beers, putting me up overnight... even when there was somewhere else for me to go! It was all pressed on me, and it made me feel great. I guess you think that I'm working for the Canadian Tourist Board! Maybe I should write to them, show them this last bit and demand some kind of royalty! I've tried to keep in touch with all of these people and now have many new Canadian friends.

You can't buy kindness, but you can show and exchange it... 'What goes around comes around!' I'll do the same for them if they come over here in the future, and have already done the same for others over here... picking up hitch-hikers and going out of my way for them, as others have done for me (one guy in Canada picked me up on his way home from work and insisted on driving me an hour past his turning, simply because I was doing what he had always wanted to do, but had never done!).

Lonely?

No way... on this 13-week trip I probably made up to 10 new friends *each day*. It was impossible not to meet people and make friends as others want to get to know you and, believe it or not, get a kick out of helping you. I know Canada is a very civilised place, but wherever you go in the world you can either be by yourself or with others.

➤ **This is your choice and your freedom... something you don't really have when travelling with a companion.**

Chapter 7

Female solo

> 6 *The woman who goes alone can start today;*
>   *but she who travels with another must wait*
>   *till that other is ready* 9

Adapted from Henry David Thoreau (1854) by Tom Griffiths (1997) to suit text.

New day, new opportunity!

For the first time in my life I'm going to have to say that this American (who wrote the quote on the previous page) has actually made a bit of sense. Furthermore, he still makes sense over a century later! The advantage of travelling solo? Well, he's hit the nail right on the head. Independence. Go when you want, where you want, with no one or nothing holding you back.

➤ So what's stopping you? Go! Off round the world, by yourself. Piece of cake. Loads of other women have done it by themselves, so why shouldn't you? You'll be all right!

Is this what you are thinking at the moment?

If so, good for you. However, as you well know, and I'm sure it's at the back of your mind at the moment... it's easy enough to say that while sitting in the warmth, comfort and safety of your room, dreaming of hot, golden, sandy beaches in places that you probably haven't even heard of, let alone being able to spell!

- Have you got what it takes?
- Are you confident enough?
- Will you enjoy it, or would you prefer to have the company of a friend for companionship and added security?
- What are you looking for in this trip?

If these are some of the questions that you've been asking yourself for a while, or are just starting to ask yourself, then I hope this chapter will be of some use to you. I want all young people who go off travelling to have an absolute ball and an amazing and unforgettable experience. However, this will only happen if you get it right from the start. It is not up to me to say to you... OK you should travel with a friend, and you over there, yes you with the striped flares and the dyed hair, you should travel by yourself.

➤ It is for you to make and take that decision and no one else.

The world of advice!

As a young lady about to go off travelling the world by yourself, you are about to discover the world of fantastic advice. Everyone you know will give you the benefit of their advice/experience whether you want it or not! You may be undergoing this at the moment... isn't it just so irritating! Your dad wants you to go off and broaden your mind, but to be careful while you are doing it. Your mum just thinks that you are going to be raped, killed or both. Your granny keeps on going on about how in her day young women would find a nice young man, settle down and hold the house together and not go gallivanting off around the world like a young hussy. But she's still given you a £5 note to go off and buy a rucksack, unaware how prices have risen since the war!

As for everyone else, well, they've seen the news clips over the past few years – the murder in Thailand, the young lady pushed off the bridge, the girl eaten by a crocodile – all high profile, all tragic, all shocking. Unfortunately this puts everyone in the mindset of being the foremost expert on the subject of young women travelling by themselves, or at all for that matter. Such news is horrific, but unfortunately things like this happen in the world, young people's lives being cut short in London, Manchester, Liverpool and Glasgow every day. So do things like this only happen to female backpackers on the backpacker trail? **NO.**

Let's put things in perspective for a moment

The point I'm trying to make is that unfortunately in life bad things happen. I've been mugged, and I'm sure a few of you out there are in the same boat. Yes it was nasty, I didn't enjoy it one bit. I was 16, and on my own in France. Shit happens! However, the press need a story, it's on the news, suddenly every female backpacker in the world is at risk.

➤ **Have you ever heard the newsreader saying... 'and finally on the news tonight, 20,000 female backpackers were said to be all well and having a fantastic time all over the world tonight, which we are all very happy about. That's all from...'.**

As I mention later on in the book, you are more likely to be mugged or have things happen to you in your own environment back in your home town, than you are abroad. The simple reason is that you are more aware of your surroundings when you are in unfamiliar territory, whereas at home you tend to become unaware of everything that is around you... because it's always there! Statistically it is safer to travel than to stay at home, purely because of the enormous number of accidents that happen around the home...

You'll be fine!

I think you're aware of what I'm getting at now. You will be fine. You will be safe. I mean, you're very unlikely to put yourself in a dangerous/compromising situation, aren't you! There are thousands of females who travel alone, just like there are thousands of blokes who travel alone. The general tip is **don't worry**, you'll meet people as soon as you get on the plane. Jane, for example, pretends to hate flying and then gets the guy next to her to hold her hand on take off. Always one for a good icebreaker is our Jane! By the time you land you'll probably have met others on the plane, if not you'll meet them at the first hostel anyway. **From then on in, you'll find that you'll never be alone unless you really want to be.**

Coming back to the independence bit, this is where you'll find your advantage lies. If you want to be by yourself, you can, and if you want to be a social butterfly, it is all too easy to bounce from one set of friends to another. Go sailing with this group, scuba diving with that one... everywhere you go you'll meet up with loads of people. Everyone is in the same boat.

The name of the game?... meeting people and having a laugh!

Wherever you go you'll find that there are hundreds of trips organised for you. At every stop and at every hostel you'll find offers for everything from whale watching, koala spotting, scuba diving, turtles hatching... to bungee jumping, rafting, sky diving, horse-riding... I could go on all day if you wanted me to... reef surfing, camping trips, beer factory tours, island tours, watersports, etc., etc., etc. Do it all! I'm getting excited just thinking about it, so I'm sure that you are too. But the main thing about it is that you'll meet loads of other backpackers on these trips too.

➤ You are all doing the same thing, so just sit back and enjoy it!

Let's cut the faffing around and get on to the useful stuff!

I hope now that you've got the confidence and conviction that it is possible for you to travel alone. It is a lot easier than most of you realise. Once you've decided that you've got this confidence to get up and get on with sorting out your travel arrangements, you'll realise that good planning will mean the difference between living your dreams, or confronting your nightmares. However, you are not indestructible, infallible, or immortal (even though it would be great if you were... you'd have all sorts of men after you!) so don't expect it all to be too much of a piece of cake, as you do still have to look after yourself.

Packing

For a good backpack, pack, divide in two, re-pack, and divide in two again. Then do a preliminary re-pack. Once packed, ask where the scales are hidden in the house, and then weigh your pack. *At this point you may well be faced with the realisation that the scales don't actually lie and you will be forced to agree with them!* Having weighed the pack don't be tempted to weigh yourself. As long as you're happy, what does it matter what anyone else thinks anyway? And if any man says any different, give him hell... he'll soon learn to keep his mouth shut and opinions to himself anyway!

Finally you should try and get your pack down to **no more than about 8kg**. You really should be ruthless at this stage and ask yourself whether you really do need three pairs of 'going out' shoes. If you've really got to ask yourself these questions you probably don't need them, so throw them out.

Trust me (how many times have you heard that from a man, eh?) when we (myself and the girls) say that you are going to collect a lot of things on the way. Your pack will get bigger, and it will get heavier. So unless you have the muscles of an Albanian goat-herder's wife, **do yourself a favour now and pack as light as possible**. The girls have devised an additional 'think about' list below to go with the one under '**Packing**', so have a look and a little think about it. If it does come to over 8kg, don't worry too much, as you'll be able to send things home en route when it gets too heavy. That said, don't be put off collecting those little momentos, as a few years down the track they are the reminders that will bring it all flooding back to you! Happy days!

Do you have a backpack?

If the answer is no and you don't know much about them, and the thought of lugging one around sounds as appetising as a snog with Andrew Lloyd Webber... don't panic! There are actually backpacks designed for women which you might prefer (see 'Packing' where I talk about 'The one that converts into a holdall/suitcase on page 21). Do remember that you have to carry it with you all the time, so make sure you shop around for something that you find comfortable, and which isn't going to fall apart on you a couple of weeks into the trip. Don't be fobbed off with your dad's old Scout, heavy duty, green, canvas rucksack. Sure, you can throw it under a car doing 100mph and it'll survive, but as soon as it gets heavy it'll hurt your back and you'll regret taking it.

What tips have we got for you?

Confidence

Every girl that I have met travelling has exuded confidence. Whether they have it or not, they showed it. If you are a naturally confident person this will be natural for you anyway. You'll ask for things, go up to people and introduce yourself, join in, find your way around, and damn well get whatever, or to wherever, you want. If you are not a naturally confident person, you will be doing exactly the same, except that you'll be doing all this a bit slower than the 'naturals'. But don't worry, because the change in you will happen. **You don't need to force it, it just happens.**

The environment is totally different; everyone's attitudes are different and you'll soon learn by what everyone else does. It's a very harmless transformation that you'll find will come very naturally to you. **Your confidence is there inside, it just takes a relaxed and unpressured lifestyle for it all to come out.** Additionally, a change from your usual surroundings/mates tends to help. From the age of maybe 11 upwards you will be in groups of friends. Maybe you were one of the 'leaders' of the group, or a 'follower' in the group. Whichever it was should be of no difference... that was all 'kids stuff'! When you travel, age, race and height on the social ladder make absolutely no difference.

You will very rarely wear make up. Sometimes you may go for a week without looking in a mirror. Vanities go, weight becomes irrelevant and looks become so much less important. Suddenly people take you for who you are, not what you look like, or for who you pretend/would like to be. This seems to be the big lesson that people learn. The result is more confidence in the person that is really inside you, and so a stronger character.

In terms of travelling, you'll walk confidently in the street, be assertive, make decisions, be spontaneous, etc., etc.

Always look as though you know where you are going, even when hopelessly lost. You are therefore less of a target as you look less vulnerable. You will exude confidence, to the point that it will smack people in the face from 20 yards!

Fake wedding ring

Essential item. The most important item. Get one! It doesn't have to be an expensive one, in fact make sure that it isn't worth anything. All you need is an accessory which can be used in pretence if needed. As long as you don't have any superstitions, then simply slipping it on in times of need does the

The 'no-go' zone

job perfectly. A wedding ring, a few blatant lies and a bit of acting will get you absolutely everywhere and always out of trouble. Your husband will be meeting you at the 'next stop'. Your husband is just 'over there', as you confidently walk over to some nice young man/men who you may/may not have met, sit down and, with ease, move out of a sticky situation. The fact that you are seen as another man's property might help to keep unwanted attention at bay. Very useful, and imperative that it accompanies you at all times.

Leave a record of your stay

And I don't mean by pulling every available man in the building, or by smashing all the crockery in a drunken impression of your favourite Greek night in Swanage! In all the hotels, hostels and backpacker places there is always somewhere where you can leave some sort of record of the date of your visit, and even an indication of where you are off to next, and with whom. Try

Make your mark

not to make strict plans to meet up with friends or relatives en route from home before you go, as you will find invariably that your plans will change. You may then find it difficult/impossible to be there through no fault of your own. If you're late and various people/relatives are expecting news back home, you really will cause a lot of unnecessary anxiety and worry.

I hope this backs up what I have said in the section 'Keeping in touch' under '**Parents**'. These are good reasons for not sending postcards at regular intervals, and for not promising to send letters and postcards on certain dates. If you forget, or leave your parents waiting for news, then they'll only think the worst. You may be off exploring tropical islands with no post office for hundreds of miles... but do they know that? No! They simply think you are lying dead in a ditch somewehere. **'I'll be in touch' normally does the trick... especially if you are!** As for meeting up with people en route and keeping in touch, there is no excuse nowadays with email and you can also use the 'Post Restante' (outlined under 'Parents') and the American Express postal service. Even if you are not getting on with your folks very well at the moment, please make the effort to keep in touch.

Asking for help

The most obvious thing to do? Then why do people always wander around saying 'We'll find it in a minute, I know it's around here somewhere!' Is it just a British thing where we're too polite to stop people and ask for their help? The Americans are very good at doing this... maybe this is the price we have to pay for a culture! Asking for help saves so much wasted time. If I turn up in a town, starving, but lost... I usually go to a bar/restaurant and ask the barmen and waiters where they would go for something to eat/drink. They'll usually point you in the direction of where all the young people tend to 'hang out', again meaning that you're not in the wrong place and so you don't stick out as a tourist. Often in these situations you'll find yourself invited to parties, etc. as you are recognised as a newcomer to the area.

Ask for everything... you'll never miss out. And if you don't ask? You don't get! It'll also save you a lot of time. I know you'll have all the time in the world, but that's not the point!

Be aware of potential hassles and how to deal with them

If you are aware of them and somehow expect them, then the theory is that they shouldn't be too bad if they happen. On the odd occasion in developing countries you will be exposed to the crush of touts, hustlers, salesmen and children offering you everything from a room, to food, watches, bracelets, drugs and sex... well anything really! Once you've had a bit of travel experience under your belt, you'll find the situation fairly easy to deal with.

However, if you land in Delhi, Bangkok or Marrakech fresh from 'Jolly Old England', totally unprepared, boy are you in for a shock! At this point you may well be grateful for reading **'Tips, hints and problems**, Chill out!' (page 147)', and 'Locals' (page 162). If not, you may well have the desire to beat a retreat faster than the Allies at Dunkirk, and jump on the first plane home... it happens!

The other way to deal with hassles of course is to 'bite the bullet' and go for it. It can be very daunting for the first time, but is more harmless than it seems. It is the fact that you are surrounded by a lot of people who think that because you are from a developed country that you have a lot of money. When you think about it, you may well find that you do have a lot of money in relation to the great majority of them.

If going round the world avoid too much culture shock by getting some travel experience under your belt and warming up in countries such as Australia, USA, and Europe first. Go anti-clockwise round the world first if in doubt

Try and put it in perspective – usually helps me

The tugging at you from all directions is just a way of them getting your attention, as they don't speak your language. All the 'babbling' in a foreign language, which is as far from the Grade B in GCSE French you got as you can be, is only their 'business talk', discussing the deals they could give you. However, your paranoia in these situations forces you to believe that they are plotting your demise! They're not savages you know, they're hardly likely to talk about assassinating you in front of everyone! **Nevertheless you must try and avoid being ripped off, and watch for pick-pockets who take advantage of these swarming crowds.**

You will not be harmed in situations like these, they are just after your business. If you are struggling and finding any situation like this a bit too overwhelming or frightening, take a few deep breaths and chill. Take your backpack, find a safe place to sit down just away from the hustle and bustle and just take a few minutes to sit and watch. The easiest way to deal with any situation is to try and understand it. So take your time. However, when ready to move do take care to check the situation out properly before getting in taxis, and check out the room before you pay for it. If you don't like it, go elsewhere. Don't be afraid to pay more for your own peace of mind.

Blondes beware!

… because a lot of men in some countries tend to be fascinated by your hair. In countries where there are very few/no blondes, a lot of men will have no qualms about coming up to you and touching your head. Jane, for example, also found that many felt that they had the right to get you in to bed, and would not take no for an answer… you know what I mean, ten to two at your local night-club as the slow songs come on!

I shouldn't really joke around the subject as **a lot of blondes feel very intimidated and threatened in areas such as Africa, India, South East Asia and the Middle East**. You're bound to. In India, Jane was unlucky enough to travel with another blonde. It did turn out to be a bad experience… a lot of staring, touching and this fascination for sex. She thinks it had a lot to do with the stacks of Western porn that they get over there, leading many men to believe that they can simply walk up to a white woman and she will jump into bed with them. Whatever the reason, be aware of this.

Remember that being from a developed country you have a freedom that many women don't and therefore the men will often be interested in you. Respect their culture, as you are in their country. According to Jane, 'It is not especially frightening, just bloody annoying! Ignore them is the best advice, as trying to stop them doing it is just seen as a "come on".' You'll probably find yourself travelling with a group of people anyway. But, if in doubt, don't be proud, just hook up with some people for a while. No worries!

Victorian maid shows ankle to chimney sweep scandal!

Remember that this still happens in a lot of countries, especially the Muslim ones, so wrap up! Your G-string and skimpy bra top may look fantastic on the beaches of the South of France, but may not go down too well upon entering some of Asia's most sacred buildings... the Taj Mahal being a classic example! Also avoid topless sunbathing, shorts, sleeveless tops, hot pants, etc. in certain countries. Do get advice before you go and from the locals and hostels while

Meet the locals...

you are there, and cover up to avoid any hassles. You are a guest in their country, so it is always polite to abide by the rules. In hot countries, cover up with loose-fitting cotton garments to keep cool... or sweat like a pig (do whatever you feel most comfortable doing!). I know that all this will seem extremely Victorian to you, and perhaps unfair, but then you must realise that you are only visiting... their women have to live with it.

Breasts

Can shock, even in this country. Similarly, for me to use it as a title like I have above will cause a few raised eye-brows. Just as you wouldn't walk around with them on display in any high street store, shoulders and legs exposed can cause equal discomfort, anger and embarrassment in many countries. Conservatism is the word of the day, especially when you come up against any officials, and definitely when applying for visa extensions, at borders, etc. Sorry girls!

OK enough said, let's conclude this little bit Tom

Cathy is blonde and spent some time out in some Middle Eastern countries. Having spoken to her, she spoke some words of wisdom! She seemed to encounter most of the things a young female traveller might come up against and so here are her 'top tips'.

Cathy's Top Tips!

DO:
- wear a sober coloured headscarf
- try and blend in as much as possible
- be aware of what's going on around you
- be cynical of helpful strangers, especially male ones
- ask women for directions/help
- on trains and buses:
  1. sit near/next to a woman
  2. if you can afford it, take the more expensive option as it will tend to carry a better class of person and so be more hassle free

- take Tampax and contraception with you – sanitary towels are cheap and readily available, but Tampax are expensive and harder to find
- assume everyone is trying to con you – they probably are, especially in the tourist areas!
- take your Walkman – on long journeys it is a great way of being in your own world, but it also means that people can't engage you in conversation.

Cathy's Top, Top Tip!

If someone tries to touch you up in the street, don't be afraid of making a fuss, especially if you get your arse pinched, etc. Accidents do happen as you have to brush past people, so don't get paranoid. However, if they do try and take advantage, scream and shout at them. As well as feeling better yourself, they will be embarrassed and may learn that it's not acceptable behaviour.

DON'T:
- show any bare flesh – except the unavoidable; whatever the weather, cover shoulders, legs, stomach and chest
- wear tight clothes (see Nina's comments later) as they are hot and grab attention.
- attract attention with clothes or behaviour (except the last DO before)
- make eye contact in the street
- eat what you consider to be dodgy meat – it's better to be safe than sorry... one way of avoiding food poisoning

- forget that countries such as the Middle East are known for their hospitality, i.e. by being totally paranoid you may miss out or offend; use your judgement
- put your camera or wallet/purse on show; keep them secure and hidden
- rely totally on guide books; they are good for guidance, but are quickly out of date.

What are work opportunities like?

Well would I surprise you if I said that work opportunities for female backpackers are a lot better than for us men... or am I just being a jealous male chauvinist! I don't hear any moans of sympathy out there, but then we probably don't deserve it anyway! Always ask at hostels that offer very good/sought-after jobs which are great if you can get them. Agencies are always a good bet if you intend to stay in a place for a while. Telesales are mundane but can pay well. Avoid door to door, as you'll usually get ripped off. Australia is one of the best places to find work.

Australia

Are you going to Australia? It has excellent medical care via 'Medicare'. It is good for things like smear tests, as they test once a year there... so use it. Get a Medicare card on arrival. When I had the stitches put in my head, it cost a fair bit. Without a Medicare card I had to wait until my claim went through

If travelling alone, try and choose loose, comfortable clothes. Apart from the practicality of it, it avoids outlining your body, and so also avoids you being subjected to unwanted male attention... which I'm lead to believe 'can be more than a little boring' according to Nina... she must have met a few of my mates!

Chapter 8
Going with a friend

A pleasant companion reduces the length of the journey — **Pubilius Syrus (50 BC)**

Are your budgets similar?

This is quite easily the most preferred way of travelling... a couple of friends from school or college decide that it's about time they went off to see the big wide world. You've talked about it a lot, dreamt about it, and the time is getting near. The best thing about travelling with a friend is that you really do motivate each other, which is a very good thing. You may well have been in the situation where countless other friends have stated an intention of coming with you, even a few... 'yeah, of course I'm definitely coming', and others who have talked about going off to see other parts of the world with other friends of yours. But at the end of the day you know that they are only being the 'impotent parrot'... 'all talk and no action!'

Again we're back onto my brother Mat's wise old saying about the '**doers**' and '**talkers**' in this world... these kind of people are 'talkers' and will spend their life 'talking' about all these fantastic things that they are going to do. And then in 30 years' time they will be the ones that rabbit on to people like us about the things they have always wanted to do, but never quite did for some reason or another... for which they'll have an adequate number of excuses. But inside I'm sure they'll really feel that they missed out on this opportunity in life... one which you're about to take!

➤ OK, so we've established that you and your friend(s) are 'doers' and that you are about to do something a little bit more adventurous than have a two-week drunken spree in Corfu with the lads/lassies.

If one, or both, of you are very nervous about doing the trip, I think you'll find that the determination of not letting your partner down will weigh quite heavily on your mind. This is actually a good thing and it drives you both on to get organised, earn the money, and go. For myself and Tony, we bought the ticket early (which we found was great for our motivation), and then worked our botties off to earn the money so as to not let the other down... He sold his nuts and his pride and joy (chestnuts and his VW Beetle that is!) and I ate seven months' worth of Big Macs, chicken burgers, fries and doughnuts on my breaks at Maccy D's!

What do we think of travelling with friends then?

Well, because you're doing the trip together, really make it a trip together, i.e. don't let one of you do all the legwork because he/she is better at finding deals/maths/talking to people/shopping, etc. If you do it all together you will both know exactly what is going on, and so feel in control. This will save hassles later on, especially with situations like... 'well you're the one who persuaded the travel agent to send us to Baghdad!' Between you, you'll be able to reach some sort of compromise as to where you'd like to visit, when, what you'd like to do, etc. You'll no doubt find that you'll agree on everything anyway, especially if it's been the topic of conversation between you for a while. However, do take your time at this stage to get everything out in the open and discuss things that may become problems, especially if there are more than two of you travelling together.

If you've read **Decisions** already, you'll know what I'm talking about. So time to jump in with:

Get to the travel agents and thrash out some ideas. If you are the one who is doing less of the talking because you feel happy to do what the others want to do, don't! Remember that it is your trip, too, so make sure you have your say and then work out some sort of compromise, as you'll only regret it later... something that you obviously don't want.

Is (are) your companion(s) the right choice?

Have you even thought about this? Many don't, as you tend to think, 'Well they've been my friend for quite a few years now.' But... is there something about them that annoys you intensely? Remember that you're about to spend virtually 24 hours a day travelling with them for however many months. There is a saying that 'You really don't know someone unless you've lived with them!' Well I've just thought of a similar one...

> 'You really don't know how annoying your friend's sleeptalking, fussiness, smelly feet, bad breath, drunken misbehaviour, major untidiness/picky tidiness, boring stories, lousy jokes, chronic flatulance... are... until you've travelled with them!'

Looking back at that last bit... it just about sums me up. God knows how Tony put up with me!

Girlfriend/boyfriend?

I'm sorry to say that if you are planning a 'big trip' together, **beware**. I really do mean this in big neon letters with sirens going off and the works. If you are really keen on that person then it is a very big risk to take. The number of couples I've met, i.e. not just heard about, but **actually met**, who have broken up mid-trip has amazed me and **actually put me off ever travelling with a girlfriend**. Mind you, if she was loaded and it was a

Travelling with Tony!

first-class trip around the world to places I'd like to go, with all my spending/going out included... then I might be persuaded to think about relaxing this rule... but only once mind! The variations on 'going out' range from anything from a couple of months to the 'seriously dangerous' couple of years. For some reason, it doesn't seem to work.

BUT I'm not going to put a dampner on it too much (if I haven't already!), as I've met loads of couples who've been fine and who've had a great time. In fact the intrepid Helena has done this a couple of times and has the opposite view from me... so there we go. However, she does reiterate the point that I made that if you are keen on the person, it is a very big risk to take. So think really carefully. So what am I trying to say?... well, I'll be totally honest with you, it is a difficult one, so I'll throw you a few little thought provokers for you to think about.

➤ **OK, so what problems are there, and why should you be careful?**

- It's a lot of money spent, which tends to weigh heavily on your mind when you are having problems.
- Everyone else you meet seems to be single and having a wild time.
- Because of No. 2, you can be seen as 'the couple', and if you're not careful you can be left out of a few things... this may annoy you a bit and you may then start blaming your partner for something which may not be their fault, leading to tension and then seeing only the bad things in them!
- You may prefer to take a double room for more privacy; however, sometimes this may not be possible, so you may find you are the only

couple in a dormitory. The problems occurring in No. 3 or any strains at all may well become apparent to your room mates, who although they try their best may not be too subtle about the fact that they know. This may cause you further discomfort and problems.

- You will be spending 24 hours a day with each other, for the whole duration of the trip. Have you ever done this before? Many couples tend to work extremely hard right up to the departure point, taking all the overtime possible to earn the money, and so hardly see each other. They then look forward to going away and spending some quality/romantic time with each other. Once away, the first part of the trip is great, finally spending time together. However, after a while the novelty can wear off, and it grows increasingly tiresome – this is when the problems begin.

- You are thousands of miles away from home and from the support and advice of friends, forcing you to sort out your problems or face a massive phone bill!

However, there is a famous saying, probably from some equally famous person, **'Que sera, sera'** – **'If it was meant to be, then it will be'**. I'm a firm believer in this, and I don't think that I should be the one to discourage travelling with your partner, because it can be a very enjoyable way of seeing the world. I suppose it is also a great way of getting to know your partner better. I just want to make sure the warning signs are out there, plain to see in black and white, so that you have a serious think about what you are about to do.

With a friend/some friends?

If you've read the above, then you pretty much know what I am about to say. If you haven't, give it a quick once over. In fact, to be honest, not much really needs to be said. The fact that you have decided to go with these people is an indication of your liking and trusting of them. But it is worth having a quick think, as there is always the possibility of a fall out... 'His repetitive annoying laugh', 'Her exaggerated stories', etc.

> ➤ **If you have got intensely annoyed about one of these things with one of your prospective travel partners, you need to seriously consider RIGHT NOW what 24 hours a day will be like with this person. Will it drive you nuts?**

Or maybe your conversation is only held together by your taste in men/women... or both! This could soon run dry, and there's nothing worse than travelling with a companion with no conversation, well... maybe a naked sweaty sauna with your gran and the female members of her over-80 Bridge Club... but this surely comes a close second! If you can be honest with yourself and others about this, then it will be better for you all in the long run, but don't be so honest as to cause a major bust-up... diplomacy is the order of the day! You'll regret it if this ends up ruining your trip and, if you do end up going your separate ways while you are overseas, you will also regret having had a major bust-up with a good friend. It does occasionally happen, so it's worth giving a bit of thought to it now while your mind is on it and you have the privacy of your own thoughts.

> It is definitely better to go into these things with an open mind and with everything that really has to be said actually said, and then forgotten about. As I mentioned earlier, get everything out on the table now while you can and you are in the right frame of mind to deal with it sensibly as, the chances are... that it, whatever 'it' is, will rear its ugly head later. For many of you this may be extremely difficult, but it is something you MUST do before you finally choose your travel partner(s) and go spending your hard-earned cash on tickets.

Are your budgets fairly similar?

There really is nothing worse than feeling guilty about tucking in to a nice juicy bit of shark steak, or octopus, or feeling how your palate copes with the delights of crocodile accompanied by one of the local wines... as your travelling buddy tiresomely ploughs through another omelette and asks for another glass of water. You may both indicate politely to each other that you don't really mind, but it does put a bit of a dampener on the occasion! Similarly, as you fall into your room and wake your pal up at goodness knows what hour, completely off your box from excessive drinking, for the sixth time that week (and it's still only Saturday!)... when he/she had to retire early as he/she couldn't afford to go to the club with the rest of you – this may settle on the nerves a bit, and start to ruin the trip a smidgeon. So do bear it in mind.

So... that's the general idea of the sort of ground rules you should think about making, even before you go. You should also establish who should send off for what, find out about this and that, etc. **Why not think about writing the ground rules down on the back of a beer mat (depending on how drunk you are!), signing it, then putting it away and finally forgetting about it?** It will all be said and done, and noted in the back of your mind... for future and emergency use only! The beer mat will then be one of those momentos that you will find in a few years' time, pull out, and have a laugh at. 'Those were the days, eh?'

Scouts and brownies... be prepared!

Ground rules sorted out, tickets bought, money earned, strategy worked out... you'll find your departure date will fly upon you quicker than the runs after a dodgy vindaloo! They say you should learn from your own and other people's mistakes, which I suppose is what a lot of this book is really about. So, don't go in blind, **do make sure you are prepared**... for instance, make sure you can put your tent up and take it down and that it's all there in the bag before you leave.

Making ground rules. What I'm leading up to is that it is always a good idea to establish some basic ground rules over a few beers some night... serious ones like:

1. It's okay to go your separate ways for a few days if agreed by all parties concerned, or even for good if you really don't get on. If you've caught the gist of what I've been saying so far – that travelling is easy, too easy sometimes – it is very easy to meet further up the road somewhere at a certain time. This will give you all/both a bit of time and space apart.

2. Agree to have some sort of meeting or something, so that you can air your views if you are unhappy about anything. But most importantly, always agree to find a solution i.e. not to argue about it too much, as you'll find this pointless and a waste of time. You'll soon see that arguing solves nothing when travelling with friends, although I doubt you'll even find time or anything to argue about anyway!

Get everything said and out in the open now. Therefore, it's been said, so you can now get on with the important stuff!

➤ So get the checklists going, and everything bought and put aside. The last thing you need is a last-minute rush around (although it does get the old heart pumping!). Departure day arrives... you go... you're gone!

The advantage of travelling with someone else, especially if you are a particularly nervous pair, is that you can see what you are like just by looking at them! **You're both going through the same thing together, and you'll find that in every situation you pull each other through.** You'll soon find out all sorts of things about your companion that you never knew. Tony, for example, found out about my love for practising my didgeridoo... early in the morning... in our two-man tent! He also found out that I wasn't very good at first... was I, Tony?

Advantages

The more confident one of the two of you/your group will always be able to start conversations to get you introduced to others. If you are a two, three or more, you will find it easy to join big groups of people, or to start your own, and so become known by people wherever you go. **Exhibitionists** – if this is one of the best words in the English dictionary to describe you... then all the better! It is very easy to 'perform' double acts at the backpacker places you go to and so become known and get to meet people. We have all met them, and can still remember them and their antics! If you're that kind of person, yet not too overbearing with it, you will have a lot of fun in most of the backpacker places you go to, and make a lot of great friends.

But don't go over the top, as you'll just end up looking like Victor Pratt and his Marshmallow sidekick! You'll then get the opposite effect – of making people want to avoid you, or attracting only fruitcakes like yourself.

➤ *You will also find travelling with a partner very useful when you need to find accommodation.*

Tony and I for example would use this to our advantage if we arrived somewhere either by air, bus, or plane. One would sit looking after the bags, while the other went off in search of hotels, hostels, taxis, food, etc. This tended to work well, especially in poorer countries where you are confronted with thousands of smiley faces all promising the earth, and at a great price too (see '**Tips, hints and problems**' for how to deal with these situations). The only thing you need to worry about therefore is who is trying to rip you off and where the best place to stay really is, as you can actually go in to each place and have a look for yourself... while not having to worry about your belongings and the weight of them. You may well find that accommodation is cheaper if there are two of you sharing a room, and it will invariably be safer as you may get a lockable room, as opposed to a bunk bed in a dormitory.

Budgeting

- If there are two of you **sharing a tent** on the odd occasion, you will find that this makes the cost of accommodation minimal. In Australia, for example, if you pitch your tent in the caravan parks you'll get the use of a pool, BBQ, and good facilities for no more than a couple of quid each, plus the added security of your friendly neighbours watching over your tent for you (as they are usually OAPs who have retired there and who welcome the chance to help out some young Poms).

- In most parts of Africa you can just about pitch a tent anywhere; just be prepared to exchange food with anyone who questions your presence. Never thrust money at 'inquisitors', as you may find yourself besieged, or worse, offending someone who was just trying to be friendly.

- **You'll find it is always easier to budget with more than one person, as you will stop each other overspending, and you'll find that you can eat more cheaply when buying for two/three.**

    If you stay in a place for more than one day, do take advantage of communal fridges and cupboards. These will enable you to buy in advance for your stay, thus saving money by buying in bulk.

➤ Going with a friend or friends means that you will never be lonely, and there will always be someone there in times of trouble.

Backpackers are generally good about not nicking each other's food, but to be on the safe side always wrap/tie it up tightly in a couple of plastic bags, and then write your name and the date on the outside with a permanent black marker pen. Then stuff it into a corner at the back of the fridge. Communal fridges tend to be fairly big. If anyone is going to whip something it will usually be from the front where it is easily accessible. But this is a minor point, so don't worry too much about it.

Disadvantages?

Well there aren't many disadvantages, only that you'll spend virtually 24 hours a day with each other, and if you're the type of person who would be driven nuts by this then you should seriously think about it. The thing is that you're about to spend a fair amount of hard-earned money and you may well end up ruining your trip and a friendship. **There is a feeling of being obliged to each other, not letting each other down, etc.** This is only fair, as you'll probably have been good friends for a while before deciding to travel together, and so naturally won't let each other down. **This is why I really can't stress enough the importance of establishing some ground rules before you go**, as this can only be fair for you and your partner(s).

If you think that maybe you'd really like to have more freedom for a bit, why not go alone, and arrange to meet up with your friend(s) somewhere en route, maybe even agree to do the 'home leg' solo, or agree to the possibility of it happening.

But certainly agree to the possibility of making space for yourselves if you feel that you may need it, and be adult enough not to get offended by it. If you are good friends then you'll find that this is easy to do, and so should be no worries anyway.

However, I don't need to tell you this do I! Once this is out of the way you'll be so bloody excited about going that it'll all be forgotten.

➤ Got a companion? Got a ticket? Think ya gotta go then!

Chapter 9

Safety

' *To get attention always shout "Fire!" instead of
"Help!" as you are guaranteed a better response* '

Tom Griffiths 12.3.97 (read it somewhere, sounds good,

like it!!)

I lead a sheltered life

This is something that I am always asked a lot of questions about, and is a fairly serious subject in that it is often one of the deciding issues as to whether a person will go travelling or not.

➤ 'Yes I know that it's probably fantastic out there, all the beaches, the sun, the fun, and all of that... but will I be safe?'

Many people are put off going to places like South East Asia, South America, parts of Africa, etc. because of a fear for their safety. And now with the World Trade Center atrocity and the ongoing 'War against Terrorism', travelling the world is starting to be seen as a dangerous pastime. Indeed some of the places are a little dangerous at times for backpackers and should be avoided for your own good. Obviously I'm talking about the places that you know to be dangerous, i.e. Rwanda, Papua New Guinea, etc., not the places **you think** to be dangerous, but probably aren't, like Swindon. If you are worried about a particular country that you would like to visit, check out the Foreign Office website www.fco.gov.uk where you can find all the information you need about the countries you wish to visit. They have a 'Know Before You Go' campaign which you should investigate (website: www.fco.gov.uk/knowbeforeyougo). They have a great service where you can create your own information page on countries and they will email you country updates, which is extremely useful. There is also the option of giving their Foreign Office Travel Advice number a call, and they will tell you anything that you would like to know concerning the state of the country at the time (this and other useful numbers are in the back of the book).

It's not as dangerous as you think

I know I have touched briefly on a lot of what I am about to say on this subject already throughout the book and I hope that I'm not going to repeat myself too much, but if I do I feel that it's something which is worth repeating. Also, if I get a lot of it down here in one section then you might find it all a bit easier to swallow... and I hope believe!

Travelling really isn't as dangerous as we are all led to believe. Hundreds of thousands of young Brits leave the country each year to travel the world and it is reckoned to be safer to travel the world than to stay at home, purely because you tend to be more alert and aware of your surroundings. Unfortunately the world is scared, society is scared, everyone is scared of something.

This is why the thought of unknown places such as South East Asia, and the scary stories that we always hear about, are enough to put even the hardiest of us off. Even I was a bit sceptical when I first considered South East Asia as an option and find it incredible now, having been there, that I ever thought that at all! Travelling in most areas of the world is safe, and it is a lot easier to travel round than you think. I believe that the best thing you can take with you on your travels for your own safety is a bit of self-confidence and common sense.

Dealing with dodgy situations

Unless you are trained to stand up to attackers, and have some kind of black belt to prove it, then this is really not a good idea. Yes you may well get in a quick lucky kick or punch, but you are severely missing the point here. The point is that no matter what age, height, sex or race the attacker is, that person (with a weapon) is still a threat. If you decide to take them on, then you will end up being one of these people that gets stabbed or slashed just for the money in your pocket. They have nothing to lose, otherwise they would be doing something else.

What about your pride though?

What about living the rest of your life with 15 stitches across your face?

➤ 'Is my life worth the amount of money in my pocket?'

If you think that your life is only worth £20–30 max., then go for it... take them on! Personally, I reckon that my life is worth about the value of the UK's GDP, which is considerably more than what I will ever carry in my pocket. So what do you do?

Assess the situation

There is absolutely no shame in doing a runner from a kid with a weapon, or anyone for that matter. If you are thinking differently at this moment, you are a prat. They have nothing to lose, and at the end of the day it is very unlikely that they will ever be caught. I know of people that have been stabbed by kids as young as 8. You only have to look at the news to see that:

It's a bad old world out there. Things like this happen everyday to all sorts of people. I was mugged in France; I wasn't the first and I definitely won't be the last. If you run away from a mugger (depending on the circumstances of course) are they really going to run after you? No... they're going to get the hell out of there before the Law turns up! They're not going to run after you, tackle you to the ground, and then wrestle the money off you! However, this is for you to assess, and for you to decide. I don't want any of you coming back to me saying 'Well you said do this, so I did and got hurt!' – 'cos I didn't...

➤ At the end of the day the final decision and how you react is entirely up to you.

Put it down to experience and learn from it.

It's nothing to be ashamed of; it happens everyday, but there are a few things that you can do:

- Carry 'mugger's money' around with you in a dummy wallet – a small amount of money so that if you do get mugged you hand it over straight away with the impression that it is all the money that you have. Saves you losing all the important other stuff in your wallet.
- Make yourself less of a target; don't be conspicuous; blend in.
- Take care when walking at night; be alert and aware of your surroundings.
- Take care when walking in daylight; be alert and aware of your surroundings!

Very deliberate there... **the point that I have made previously in the book is that you are more likely to be mugged in your own town than in somewhere like Delhi, Mexico City, New York, etc**. This is simply because you are more aware of your surroundings in unfamiliar territory. In your own town you are not aware simply because you see the same things around you every day. There do seem to be more muggings in broad daylight, maybe because you are less suspecting, whereas people generally make themselves less of a target now at night. That's only my theory... but it's a thought, and backs up what I'm saying quite well.

- Stay calm, because if you panic they might panic.
- If you're not Jean Claude Van Dam, make out that you're Elmer Fudd; they may then underestimate you.
- Trouble in a bar/in the street... if it's got nothing to do with you, stay away, don't get involved (obviously depending on the circumstances). There is always someone bigger and harder than you out there. They may only seem to be 4'2", but they may be deadly at kickboxing!
- When travelling, you are number 1, you are the priority here... look after yourself and others with you. Avoid trouble, and avoid others who invite trouble.
- Running to safety is not cowardice, it's common sense... especially when you are miles from home, can't speak the language, and can easily be framed by a local with a bit of collaboration if they have something against you. In situations like these, if things are going disastrously wrong for you, don't faff around: get in touch with the Embassy asap.

Don't be flashy, be safe

- Be careful about flashing valuables around, even among fellow backpackers. Yup, I'm sorry to say it but you do get one or two arseholes, or the odd local 'infiltrator'.
- Hotel/hostel safes: do you consider them to be safe?

- Be careful about leaving things near open (or even closed for that matter) windows, especially if on street level or next to a fire escape, as thieves can easily reach in.

Ouch

- Make sure you do take little padlocks and chains. You'll then be able to chain your belongings to the bed, seats in airports/buses/trains, etc. However, if a thief really wants to get into your stuff they will – with a knife! Padlocks, pacsafes, chains, etc. are therefore only there as a deterrent and for security, stopping your pack from being whipped from where it is. So don't go overboard with the padlocks and chain, they just need to be visible. If you lose your keys to them they should be small/weak enough that you can break them yourself to get in – a good reason for buying combination locks.
- Make sure the locks work on the door to your room and that there is some kind of emergency exit out of the building. Remember that if you don't like the room, ask for a better one, after all you're the one paying for it.
- The Childers Hostel fire is a reminder to us all to check out the hostels for bars on the windows (great to keep thieves out but also impossible to get out of in an emergency) and for bunk beds up against windows. Walk away from any hostel or accommodation you feel is unsafe. The more we all do this, the more we can help to put an end to unsafe conditions in hostels.

● Be careful who you give your address to, or information about where you are staying, before you have worked out your new friend's intentions.

Again I can't stress enough how rare being mugged or having dodgy things happen to you while you're away is, but I feel that if I play on your paranoia enough you will look out for yourself and be aware and ready for anything...

Why is this guy being really friendly to me? What are his intentions? How does he know that I am British? How does he know that I have just been to Fiji? Why is he looking at my stuff? What does he want?

A little bit of suspicion will look after you and help you develop that sixth sense of yours. If strangers are worth trusting they will gain your trust in the usual ways.

Remove the airline/bus baggage identification labels as it points to the fact that you are a tourist and where you come from. Mind you, humping a bloody great backpack on your back does nothing for your disguise as 'Jo Local' and tends to give the game away somewhat – but I think you realise what I am getting at!! Do keep some identification somewhere permanently in your backpack so that if it does get mislaid somewhere it will come back 'Return to Sender'.

Also be aware of any other identifying marks on your luggage that can tell anyone anything about you. Good con men may use this as an opportunity to start up a conversation: 'Have you been to Australia yet? I stayed at a great place called Geoff's Place on Magnetic Island (having seen some sort of sticker/label on your baggage with Geoff's Place on). You may think that he's a top bloke; he's not, he's just clever, and will just bull shit, work your conversation, build up your trust, all with the intention of robbing you later.

Trouble/Thieves

There probably aren't as many out there as it might seem – the horror stories that you hear have been vastly exaggerated by the time that they reach you.

- Never risk a fight unless you have served in the SAS for at least three years, and, even then, be cautious!
- Don't look as though you are about to go for your gun!
- Whatever the situation, it is likely to be over in a short space of time and you'll never see that person again... so put it down to experience and get on with your life.
- If your bag is snatched, do think about giving chase (if they had the guts for a confrontation they would do it in the first place); they may well drop it due to the weight and you in pursuit.

However

- Don't get yourself into hotter water than you already are by running into dark/quiet areas or getting lost.
- Make sure all of your valuables are in your daypack, and get used to not letting this out of your sight (so if your pack does get nicked at least you'll have the money to buy a new one + clothes, etc.)... however, you should consider splitting your credit cards, cash, travellers' cheques, etc. between your daypack and your backpack, so if either of them does go walkabout then you are not going to be completely screwed.
- If you look after your things properly this will never happen (it is very very, very rare as it is anyway). The thing is, with all of your belongings in this little pack, you tend to look after it extremely well anyway... So don't worry too much!

➤ **Don't have nightmares!**

Why not take a quick self-defence course before you go? They are available everywhere, and do wonders for your self-confidence. I know I mention this in the '**Tips, hints and problems**' chapter, later in the book as well; it's just that I think it's so important that if I mention it twice you might take it in... I'm not just being a dozy pratt!

As I've hinted all the way through this book, once you are on the backpacker trail you will find that you are mixing with people like yourself and you will be perfectly safe. I am assuming that you all have a bit of common sense about you, and that you will learn pretty quickly how to suss people out, look after yourself, and generally become a little bit 'streetwise'. People are always joking about this expression, but we all have to learn it sometime.

I learnt it on my first trip when I was mugged. You've got to realise that I was brought up in the country, schooled in the town, but still had quite a 'quiet' childhood. As far as I was concerned 'grass' was what I used to cut in the garden with the lawnmower, 'smack' was what I used to get on my bum when I did anything wrong, 'gear' was one of the things in a car that made it go, and 'acid' was what I used to add to various rocks in my chemistry lessons to make them 'fizz'. As for nine-year-olds with broken bottles, con men with no teeth, and strangers nicking my things if I left them out in the open and turned my back... **naart in Straaatford St. Maaary boiy... naaart in moiy vyllige... cos oim a caaantry boiy aaarnt oi!**

We all make mistakes, and we all learn from them. It's just that on a big trip you are exposed to more things that will test you than you could possibly imagine. If you are aware and ready for whatever travelling can throw at you, then you will have no troubles.

> ➤ Travelling is easy and it is not as dangerous as it is made out to be. Being confident and 'streetwise' is something that you will learn, as it is not available in the shops.

> ➤ Assess each situation as it happens, keep calm, and use your judgement to make what you consider to be a rational decision. If you aim to be safe... you will be.

Chapter 10

Money and finances

'Getting money is like digging with a needle;
spending it is like water soaking into sand'
Japanese Proverb

Money makes the world go round...

How much does it cost?

One of the biggest questions that I am always asked is, '**How much did it cost, what did you spend, how did you budget for your trip?**' If I gave an answer it would only be a rough estimate as to how much my account had increased into the red, or by what my bank manageress (I must point out again what a fantastic lady she really is, extending my student overdraft in times of need, to pay for a flight here, and a ticket there...) has let me have.

> ➤ As you realise, the hard part about this financing stuff is that you are simply going to have to sit down and work out what is really viable.

I know it's not what you want to hear but that is the nasty truth, and also the 'fun' of it, if I'm allowed to use that word! Once you know roughly how much your ticket and insurance is going to cost you will need to work out your earning potential, savings, and what you'll need to buy before you go. Once you've done this, you'll realise that unless you've got a fantastic inheritance to dig into, or the trip is to be a present, you're going to have to start saving **now!**

However, as I hope you will also realise, the whole part of working to earn the money to do this trip is all part of the 'gapyear experience' and as an added bonus is loved by employers as it looks fantastic on your CV. Once you've done it, you will also find it incredibly satisfying to know that you are going to be rewarded for everything you have done in such a great way. For me, this plays a major part in the whole result of what you achieve at the end of a year abroad... Everything you did was achieved because of **your efforts**, and no-one else's. Makes you feel kind of good inside, probably the first major thing you have ever achieved in your life?... It was for me!

How to earn the money?

If you don't have it, and you want to travel let's say in January, don't hang around... get a job! Many will laugh on hearing me say that, as I haven't (compared to most of my friends) held down many jobs. However, when I have needed to work I have worked extremely hard, i.e. all the overtime possible. I have also held up to three jobs at a time. For many this is the real decider in the question of will I/won't I go, as they may have to put it off due to lack of money. Either they haven't theoretically had the capacity to earn the money, or they haven't had the real desire to go anyway.

There are also loads of other ways to earn the cash. Sponsorship and organising events/interesting fund-raising techniques should definitely be considered. If you are doing some sort of structured placement or something on your gapyear that will be to the benefit of others or a community, there are millions of pounds out there in local funds and charities just sitting waiting to be claimed by people like you. Look for the information about grant-making trusts which can be found in the *Directory of Grant Making Trusts*. Many local churches, Rotary Clubs, Lions Clubs and Round Tables will also be happy to donate money to local people taking on life-changing experiences. And remember, if you don't ask, you don't get!

Others have done things like cycle from Land's End to John O'Groats, dressed up as a human fruit machine and wandered around town dishing out donated prizes, organising raffles with other donated prizes, car boot sales, washing people's cars... generally coming up with all sorts of crazy ideas which capture people's imagination. If you show people that you are making a serious effort and have a genuine goal in mind, you will be surprised how much support you get, especially if you get the local press interested. Don't hang around... every minute you spend faffing around is time that could be spent either thinking up unique ways to earn the cash or actually out there earning it.

Remember, all this stuff looks great on your CV and is loved by universities and employers.

➤ **My theory is that if you really want to go, and if you have the capacity to earn the money, then there is no real reason why it shouldn't happen.**

After all, for myself, the motivation has always been there in that I have always wanted to go. As long as I budget well enough, every £10 that I earn will support me for one to two days away in a foreign country.

➤ **With this kind of motivation it is hard to justify a smoking habit that costs about £20 a week, or going out and drinking away another £30–40 a week.**

If you hear yourself saying '£20... and the rest, Tom!' then you really should think about some serious budgeting. OK, so leaving in January for example: school or college finishes in June/July, which gives you about six months to earn a bit of money. If we base this on about £100 a week, which to a lot of you, if you are working loads of overtime, will be an underestimate anyway... you'll gross about £2,400... minimum!

How to help keep this figure up as high as possible?

Well, living at home always seems to be the best option, because unless you're earning a fantastically high wage, by the time you've paid

- your rent
- all the bills (gas, water, electricity and phone)
- and all your other living expenses

... you're going to take forever to save all that money! By living with your parents you'll be able to negotiate a minimum rent (always use the threat of living with them until you are 40... seems to work!), or in fact pay no rent at all, which is even better! Parents will try any old trick to get rid of their offspring nowadays!

So with any luck you'll have:
- free board
- a fridge always stocked up with food
- a job with loads of money coming in
- a goal to aim at
- and sweet dreams of far away places!

Nevertheless, it is always nice to contribute in some way to your parents so they don't actually feel like a hotel, and may actually be sad when you go... and I suppose be there when you get back (you never know, they might well move while you're away, and not leave a forwarding address – so don't annoy them!).

Do you have the right bank account?

As a student or a young person you are at a distinct advantage when it comes to choosing which bank you want to go with and choosing which account is best for you. Why's that then? Well, the banks want your business as they know that if you choose them and they give you a good service then you'll stay with them for the rest of your life. This is why they tempt students with loads of offers during their first days at university – maybe £50 cash (£50 worth of beer tokens!), a rail card, mobile phone, shopping vouchers, discount cards etc... you know the sort of thing I'm talking about – cheap gimmicks!

Unfortunately loads of people are sucked in by these and choose their bank because they went for the shiny plastic quacking mobile, the chance for some free beer or the once-in-a-lifetime opportunity to go backstage with 'N Sync (sold me!). Daft eh! It is vitally important that you take time to choose your bank and the right account, even if your bank has looked after your families' accounts since the Ice Age and gave you a porcelain piggy bank you still lovingly call 'Chuckles' when you opened your account with them aged six. There is no law that says that you can't change banks or account, especially now when you need to have one that will help you save and look after your cash before, during and after your travels.

Things you want to be looking for:
1. Things which help you with your finances before, during and after your travels, e.g. with savings, getting foreign money, etc.
2. An internationally recognised bank. The Co-operative Bank of South Central Shropshire might not have much clout with some of the big boys when you need to get things done in a hurry.

3. A bank and an account which seem to understand why you need the account – i.e. not just to make them money! This is why it is vital that you shop around and see what is out there.

When choosing a bank account:
1. Do not choose the one with the horniest cashiers in the high street (those outfits... grrrr!).
2. Do not choose on 'gimmick rating' alone.
3. Do not go with the one you think is the coolest.
4. Do not go on anyone else's advice. Shop around as these guys handle your money and so have a say in your future – so choose wisely!

To help you out there is a comparison chart of all the different 'gapyear bank accounts'/offerings for young travellers on gapyear.com which can be accessed directly through www.gapyearbankaccount.com.

Tax

- **If you're not obliged to pay it, make sure you don't.** You may well be told that you'll get a refund at the end of the tax year, i.e. in April (as it runs from April to April). Fantastic you may think, but don't be fobbed off by this, as this money is no good to you if you are halfway around the world by that time! If you are earning money for travel, make sure you get it all before the plane takes off.
- **If you are a full-time student** you will find that you are not liable for tax, and should sign the appropriate tax redemption form (P32). If you are going to earn less than the limit (at the time of writing this was about £4,535), you will not be taxed either. You will only pay National Insurance Contributions, which are fairly minimal anyway.
- **If you are taxed, you must get your employer to sort out the correct tax code for you.** You should then be refunded what has been taken off, and so given back what is due to you. If you end up returning from your trip to find a refund from the Inland Revenue of £50 waiting for you, it may well be a bonus to buy some beer or new clothes, but you will regret how far that money could have got you in Asia, South America or Africa, for example. A long way! You'll probably use it to pay off some debt or other. If you've earned it, I say... use it!
- **If you have to pay tax,** then I do apologise for harking on at the wonders of not paying it, and I wish you luck in saving the money to travel.

Local currency

Getting ripped off when changing money nowadays is very rare, especially with those friends of yours Thomas Cook, American Express (AMEX) and your

It is always sensible to arrive in a country with a small amount of the local currency if possible (£20+). This will save you the hassle of trying to find a local currency exchange, and will possibly save you money with the airport/hotel commission charges. It may also save you getting ripped off by a local 'currency exchange' as soon as you arrive before you realise that your pound will in fact actually get you 5,000 blags, instead of the 500 you got from the one-eyed 'currency man' in the street who swore that he'd met Princess Diana, and had amazingly been to where you live in England on his last visit there! Unfortunately for you it was late, you had no money for a taxi, and so you had to swallow your scepticism and take his word for it!

'flexible friends'. Years of experience of people getting ripped off with money has created a very strong and safe system for carrying money around the world. In fact (as I shall elaborate on later), AMEX is extremely efficient if things go wrong, and also offer its fantastic postal system for all of its customers... wherever they are in the world.

Changing money

Like everything nowadays, shop around. Back at home, before you go, weigh up the banks and their rivals to get the best deal for you.

- **Ask your bank what's the best deal that it can do for you.** Mine, for example (at the time of writing), gives me free travellers' cheques with my student account and will change the money back free of charge. When changing into foreign money, again, it will charge no commission. And to be totally honest, that is perfectly all right with me!
- If you know when you are going to leave the country, **why not ask them if it is worth buying your currency now or later**... as they'll be able to tell you if it is appreciating or depreciating at the time. On the eve of your departure it may be worth jotting down what the currencies are worth over

here for all the countries you are going to, so that when you arrive you will have some sort of immediate idea, which will help you to settle in easier.

- **When you land in these places miles away from the comfort of your local high street, the same rule applies**… shop around! You have the time to do so, so you might as well use it to try and save yourself some money.

- **If changing small amounts, check the commission.** The rate may be good, but the company may take a percentage above a certain figure, and a fixed amount below, e.g. £2 minimum commission, which is a lot if you are only changing £10. There are always many companies who will change money. In developed countries you will have no problems, but beware in less developed countries, as these guys will rip you off if you don't treat them confidently enough.

- **If you think they are in the process of ripping you off**, quote to them what you think is a better deal, and then **walk out** if they say no… you can always return if you can't get a better deal elsewhere. If you are confused, get them to write it all down on a piece of paper before you hand over your cash so you know exactly what deal is being put in front of you.

- The other option you'll find yourself being offered in many of the poorer countries, is the **black market**… you do get a good rate, but it is illegal. Again, circumstances will usually determine what you do, just be fully

Always find the best deal

8

aware of what you are letting yourself in for and the consequences... as well as being illegal, in many places it is used as a ploy to target a mugging victim (as they know exactly how much money you have!).

Handling cash

Do be aware at all times when dealing with your money out in the open. Is there anyone watching you? When handling large amounts of money, there is a temptation to count it there and then. The best advice is to try and handle it as though there is very little money there anyway, maybe only one or two notes instead of ten (a handy skill to have). To be honest, this doesn't really need to be said, as the declining safety on our own streets gives you more than enough practice to deal with handling money in the darkest streets of India! Are you really going to get money out at night, or in isolated places?

Didn't think so.

Credit cards

If you have access to them they are a very good idea to have or to get hold of. **The advantage of them is that you have instant access to a large amount of money that will get you out of any situation, and back home if need be.** However, they do need a lot of careful looking after (see '**Tips, hints and problems**', Credit cards) as the amount of forgery that can be done with them nowadays is incredible, leaving you to foot the bill when you return. A legitimate bill will also be there when you return which leaves you with the problem of overspending.

Been there, done that! I thought that if I only used it in 'emergencies' then I would be OK. Unfortunately, when you're away for a long period of time, it is very easy to clock up a big bill without realising it... a bit here, a present there, bungee-jump, rafting, etc., etc. There is also the temptation to stick it in a cash machine to get out a few 'readies'. As Claire found out in Germany a few weeks ago... it's easy to do, especially when you don't realise that you're being charged a pound each time you use your card in a foreign ATM! On the other hand, if you're getting out large sums of money, then a pound is a very small commission to pay.

Advantages and disadvantages but...

- For peace of mind, definitely worth having. I would recommend that everyone takes a credit card with them if at all possible.
- It is even better if you can work out an agreement with your parents/a trusted friend to pay off the bills when they come in, so that you don't have to pay the monstrous interest rates charged when you finally get home.

- Some people travel with their parents' credit cards, so if there are any problems they can get home asap.
- If you don't have one, but would like one, the bank may well be able to arrange it by holding your parents' account as collateral... if your parents agree to it, that is!
- Did you also know that if you are a student many credit card companies do not charge you the annual fee for the card? Isn't being a student great... I miss it already!

International debit cards

This is one of the best ways to deal with carrying cash around the world, as it allows you to keep cash in your bank at home and then take it out of ATM machines in the foreign countries when you need it... in the local currency. Solves all sorts of problems with having to carry cash around, getting it changed, etc., etc., etc.

What is an international debit card?

Basically it's your normal cash/switch card that you use over here, except that they paint a couple of extra logos on it, and it suddenly becomes a cash/switch card that you can use overseas in exactly the same way as over here, i.e. pop it in to cash machines in the wall to get money out of your account (10,000 miles away) and swipe at the check-out to buy stuff. The logos are simply the Cirrus, Maestro and Visa signs (depending of course on which bank you have and which systems they are linked to).

Simple to use?... YES!

How to use it

- Go to any bank machine overseas and look at the choice of logos.
- If your logos match (Visa, Cirrus, etc.), you can use the machine to withdraw money in the local currency.
- If you are in a shop overseas and you spot the Maestro logo (or whatever your corresponding one is for your bank), you can use your card as a switch card.
- Basically, with both of the above methods, it will only work if you have money in your account at home, as it debits it straight out.

International debit cards are free

All you have to do is ask at the bank and allow time for them to replace your card, as they simply change your existing card for one of these (depending on whether you are eligible with the type of account that you have).

Some important points

- Everytime you use your international debit card you'll pay 2 per cent or a minimum charge of £1.50 (at the time of writing). Therefore, on anything up to £50 you 'theoretically' lose money, so don't take small amounts out… if travelling with friends, why not take out the first £50–100 worth, and then they reciprocate it somewhere down the line?

- If you think about it (carrying on from the last point), it is a great way to change money as you are paying a very small commission and you are getting the 'competitive' rate of exchange at the time.

- Ensure your card is in good condition before you go; if not, swap it for a new one (free to do so), so you don't have the hassle of it not being able to swiped or be read. Make sure you have a legible signature which is as close to your normal one as possible. At the moment my bank card is no way near my signature, which seems to change as often as I change my pants (12 times per year)… and I have had problems all over the place, and that is here in the UK! So, to avoid even more hassle overseas, make sure you leave with a good card with a good clear signature.

- Don't lose your card. Oh yeah, great bit of advice Tom! But it is a serious point. These cards have to be dealt with back in the UK, which doesn't help if you're stuck out in the middle of Peru and are worrying about paying for the donkey trek you've just endured! Another good reason for you to sign over your account to a responsible person back in the UK (preferably parents) as, if problems like this happen, they can easily be sorted out for you.

Travellers' cheques

Thomas Cook, American Express (AMEX) or Visa? Well, again I really can't tell you which is the best; it is something you'll have to look into to see which suits your needs best. I have always used Mr Cook and he has always done me very well. For students, the travellers' cheques are free anyway through your bank and, as said above, you can always change back what you don't use free of charge, something which they all seem to do now anyway.

But of course I am saying this on the assumption that when you return you will have some money to change back. Get real Tom! **We all know that we come back totally skint having either:**

a) run out of money two days before and lived off virtually nothing, with the hope that the food on the plane will bring you round and make you look not quite as hungry as you really are when you meet your parents at the airport. And anyway, the reason that you ran out of money is because you suddenly realised that you hadn't bought your mum anything, and that she might possibly kill you if you dared to return empty handed… as you get your excuses together as to just why only one of their postcards had arrived (the one you sent the day after you left the UK!) OR

b) realised that you are going home and that what you have left in your pocket will only convert back to about £6.50. However, in terms of the 'tuk' currency of the back of beyond, or wherever you are, that money makes you a virtual millionaire. You therefore get totally ratted, and blow the lot! However, this somewhat deviates from the subject of travellers' cheques...

Advantages of travellers' cheques

- Well, they are very safe for a start, which is what you really must consider as your main priority if travelling big distances with a large amount of money.

- They are also fairly easy and quick to replace, as long as you keep the carbon separate and the other copies with a trusted friend. If this means your family, all the better.

- AMEX travellers' cheques also offer other advantages as well as being useful and reliable – such as the postal service where they will hold post for you for three months.

    I must admit though, after seeing the advert for AMEX about the guy who had his holiday saved because he had American Express, I was quite sceptical. However, since talking to Helena about them, my attitude has changed. While in Lima, Peru, she was conned out of her cheques. When she went to American Express for help, she got £500 immediate compensation AND some mail that was waiting for her from one of her friends. Bargain!

- **If you take them in a strong currency,** such as American dollars (not always best to take good old British £££££s) **you should be able to maintain the value of your money wherever you go in the world.** This is something you should discuss with someone at your bank well before you go. Find out what they advise you to take. If they do advise you to take dollars, for example, and you know that you are getting a lot of dollars to the pound at the moment, watch to see what they do. If it starts to fall, maybe you should think about buying. If it continues to rise right up to the day of your departure, all the better for you! The thing is, if you are changing a lot of money, these little changes may make a bit of difference. It might not but, at the end of the day, as long as you don't feel that you have missed out then you will go away happy.

Disadvantages

Not many really. The only thing that you have to watch out for is that you don't pay too much commission.

- You often get lower rates than for cash.

- If countersigned they are useless. Therefore don't start to countersign until you are absolutely positive that you are about to change them for cash. If you change your mind... you can't, as other places won't accept them if not signed in front of them.
- Beware of the '**fixed rate**' or '**percentage**' words on their signs. Sometimes if you are only changing a small amount you may be charged a fixed amount and so theoretically lose out. Usually changing large amounts means that you don't lose out too much on the conversion. Is this making any sense to you? Even I struggle, and I'm meant to be an economist!

  In short, if there are a few of you, it is always best to combine if possible to change money. If you can't and you're not sure if you are going to lose out on a lot, ask the cashier to write it all down for you... 'If I give you this, how much do I get back... how much?' (Remember that in some countries you will experience that millionaire feeling for a minute as you are given 25.4 million tuks, all in huge notes. It is at this point that if you are not fully aware of it all that you may get ripped off.)

- You will also be told by the lovely lady at Thomas Cook (for example) that they have branches all over the world, and that if you go to them you won't be charged commission for changing them. Very true, this happens. The only problem is arriving in New York or Delhi with only an address. These branches can be very difficult to find and it can often be worth giving up a small bit of commission to save you long walks, bus rides, and getting lost.

Again, though, you'll soon get into the swing of changing money.
Just take your time. If, like me, you are hopeless with figures, write it all down, and find out just what you are paying out, and to whom. Banks are safe. As for private money changers, usually if they ask for your passport number to write on the back... bingo! they're OK. If after you have handed over the money they jump on the back of a motorbike and roar off into the distance, you may get the feeling that perhaps all is not well!

Final words... travellers' cheques are good, reliable and safe. They also seem to be getting better and better all the time. I will always use them, so draw your own conclusions!

Money transfer

What????? Something you've never heard of maybe? Well, I hadn't got a clue about it before I used it on my first big trip and it is something that we found extremely useful. With the ease of international debit cards, you may find that this system is now a little dated. However, read on, as it may be good for your own unique situation. So, **what is it?**

Keep the travellers' cheques' numbers separate, and then cross them off when you use them.

Ask at the bank when you order your cheques for small denominations. If you get stuck with large denominations such as $50 cheques you might find them difficult to change. The other problem is that it might give you too much money, forcing you to change it back into another currency and so losing out again on the commission.

However, the main problem I've found with this is that if you have a large number of low/similar denominations, you'll find yourself with a whole wad of $20 cheques that is impossible to keep track of. You are therefore unsure of how many you have used, or if any have decided to go walkabout by themselves! Crossing the numbers off, writing down the number of the last cheque used, or simply writing down the number of cheques that you have left, should keep you on top of it all.

Well, as it says, really. All the major banks in this country are affiliated/have links with major banks in other countries. If you intend to stay for a large part of your trip in one country on the other side of the world, you can transfer money to an account over there.

I'll give you my example to explain better

I banked and still do (bless them!) with the HSBC. Tony and I, as you will already know, intended to spend most of our trip out in Australia, maybe even to work there. We therefore worked out roughly how much money we were going to budget ourselves out there, and arranged for the HSBC to transfer a whole pile of money out to the Westpac Bank in Australia. We paid a transfer fee, of course, but found this to be less than the amount we would spend each time we had to change money. Once we arrived in Sydney, Australia, we went to the main Westpac Bank where our money had been sent. Within half an hour we had an Australian bank account and a cash card with a PIN number. This meant no worries about carrying the money around, as they had banks all the way up the East Coast of Australia with the trusty 'holes in the wall', and we earned interest as well. As for getting a job, the wages were paid straight in with no hassles of opening temporary accounts (difficult to do if you are a tourist with all your money tied up in travellers' cheques, etc., leaving you only small amounts of money to deposit there... loads of forms to fill in!).

In terms of budgeting we thought it was great
- It meant that we knew exactly how much we could spend on our travels through the US and Pacific Islands before we got to Australia.
- We couldn't spend any of the money until we got there.
- And of course we knew how much we had to play with after arriving.

For ease, and just general peace of mind, I'd recommend it to anyone. Just think of all that time you won't spend queuing to change your money, and all the big notes you won't have to get out and look after. Simply step up to the hole in the wall and Bob is your Uncle!

What if I wait until I get there?
Well, in theory, this is what the money transfer is best used for. Having signed your account over to your parents, you can wait until you get to whatever country you want before asking for your money to be sent to you. In Westernised countries you can do it with just about any bank. However, in developing nations, you are best to go to the major banks in the capital cities.

How do I go about it?
- Ask the foreign bank if it will accept funds (if you're in a country where you don't speak the language, it might be worth asking the Embassy for their help to avoid any expensive mistakes).
- If they do, find out their address, branch, and full bank code.
- Then simply ring home with the details.
- Get your folks at home to ring you with confirmation that the money has been sent.
- After the allotted time period go in with full ID and withdraw the cash.

➤ **If you need the money quickly, then you might want to think about using either Western Union Money Transfer or Moneygram (outlined later on in this chapter).**

Always tell the truth

Points to note about money transfer (up to date at time of writing)

- All the major banks offer this service, which is virtually identical, i.e. in the fees that you pay, speed, etc.
- Only some banks will offer the service to people who have their accounts in other banks, but I should imagine that you will do it through your own bank, so who cares, eh?
- If the money sits in the foreign account for too long it might get sent back. So make sure you get your timings right. Dare I say it – another good reason for signing your account over to your parents!
- Fees have to be paid at both ends. You can pay both at this end, at either end, or both at that end. Do be careful if both fees are paid at this end (keep proof) so that you are not charged again.
- I talked above about opening up a bank account abroad. This was easier for me possibly due to the fact that I had a relative in Australia. Good old Aunty Nicky... ended up being put down as my sponsor on a whole host of forms that she didn't know about! Sponsors are great, just as long as you have their permission... 'cos not everyone is as trustworthy as me!
- Another important point about bank accounts in Australia is that there is a 'Whisper in the Wind' that some of the Australian banks are cutting down on giving bank accounts to non-residents who are there for less than a year. Having poked my nose about and asked a few awkward questions

here and there, all I got was a load of jumbled replies, yeses and nos. So all I can conclude is that may be something like this is about to happen.

Disadvantages?
There are always some, but these only really reflect on you.

- **You do really have to budget until you can reach this lump sum of money.** But is this really a bad thing?
- **If you get a foreign bank account, it can be too easy to use the bank card in the machines and so spend loads of money.** If you can control it, it can be a very useful aid to your budgeting. If not, you could end up spending freely, too quick, and then feeling miserable because, well… because you can't really survive without any money!

In my opinion the pros outweigh the cons on this one, so I'll leave it up to you to decide.

Emergency money transfer
Western Union and Moneygram boast that this is '**The fastest way to send money world-wide**'… well, one of them anyway. Western Union is the biggest and more established of the two (been around and doing this since 1871, perform about 30 million transfers a year, etc.), but they are both fairly similar as to how they operate, the fees they charge and the outlets they have. The concept is very simple. Banks are open from 9 to 5pm, Monday to Friday. In some countries, especially ones who indulge in siestas, Sangria and burrito-throwing competitions, banks may only open on every other full moon or when some local decides to rob it. In other words, there will be times when you need to get cash when the banks are closed. Pharmacies, post offices and 24-hour shops, however, are more likely to be open. Western Union and Moneygram therefore use these guys as agents and set up the transfer via them. They have tens of thousands of agents between them around the world – all you need to do is match up the nearest agents with you and the person sending you the money.

➤ If you want to get money out to you in a hurry… these are the guys to speak to!

How does it work?
Well, it's actually dead simple. If, for example, you need extra finances for whatever reason and your parents (bless them!) agree to all your demands:

- All they have to do is ring the Western Union (0800 833 833) or Moneygram number (00-800-66639472) (for local numbers outside the UK, visit the websites westernunion.com and moneygram.com). They will then be guided to the nearest of the agent locations worldwide... making it possible for your parents to do it even if overseas on business.

- The sender then takes the money to the agent, fills out a form, pays the service fee and receives a receipt with a control number. Your parents will then inform you of the transfer.
- You will then head off to your nearest agent, provide identification and pick up the money.

If you prefer, you can secure the transfer by putting in an identification, such as a question like your Mum's maiden name, granny's dog's name, or naming the greatest football team that has ever graced this planet... to which of course you would say 'Ipswich Town Football Club'!

It really is as simple as that!

- All operators speak English (as well as their national language), and it is all done by computer systems so that the money can literally be sent and picked up in minutes.
- Furthermore, most of the agents are in places which are either open 24 hours, or at any rate later than the usual 9–5 Monday–Friday, so you are even less restricted in your access to the system.
- The money will be converted immediately at the rate of the moment, (the rates being very competitive), so you won't have to worry about converting it all into the local currency.
- Be aware that the agents vary from pharmacies to small money-changing companies operated by locals. This means that they don't technically work for either Moneygram or Western Union. If you do have any problems, get in touch with the mother companies. You should also be wary of paying the fees twice. If your parents have paid all the fees, then you won't have to. To prevent this, just ask and keep copies of all the transaction details.

These are definitely the numbers you should be putting down in the list of useful numbers to give your parents when you head off.

➤ **NB: Even though I have written this down under the heading of 'emergency money transfer', you may well find that for your own preference, ease, and peace of mind that this may be the best way for you to handle your finances. It is a very reliable and proven system, and so it should definitely be considered. Leave a large amount of money with your parents to be forwarded to you when you get to the other side of the world... helps you to budget no end!**

For your ease you might well think of signing your bank account over to one of your parents, or a trusted friend. If there are any problems while you are away they can be dealt with immediately, rather than left to fester and get worse. These things won't go away just because you have, and they'll make a lovely nightmare end to your trip. Get them sorted at the time... by your parents. Easy, eh?

Parents

So important that I've written a full chapter on them! However, in this case they can be very useful to help you with your finances.

- Free board before you go, if lucky.
- Fridge full of food!

Don't knock these until you've missed them! Those of you who have will appreciate just what I mean by this. However, it is always nice to contribute to both of these... it may make them a bit more responsive to those pleas for cash later on!

While we're on the subject of making life easy for yourself, pick the right time and see if they'll pay your credit card bill for you while you're away. The right time? Well, I find this to be that point just after they have sat down after a three-course meal... cooked by you... and washed up by you, and while they are contemplating just how wonderful you are, having washed the car, fed, washed and walked the dog, painted the house, paid the mortgage off, etc. You know the sort of thing.

Do not try the blackmail of threatening to leave home as, considering your impending trip/behaviour during your teen years, they may not give a toss... leaving you homeless. Having them help you out if possible will mean that you will not find huge interest rate charges when you get home, and you can pay it off with a clear conscience. Also, the threats from home while you are travelling about no longer paying them off will help you to budget with ease!

Carrying money

On the market there are various goods which can be bought to carry money – money belts, neck wallets, wrist wallets, or just the good old-fashioned pocket.

For myself, and many others, I use a money belt, which I use to hold my passport, travellers' cheques, documents, licences, etc. However, I tend not to wear it as it can get itchy and sweaty. It can also be a bit of a pain if it is full of things, as it tends to get too bulky. It is often advertised as that sneaky little item that you can hide away under your clothing. Very true, and on the odd occasion you will do this as the best way of hiding your valuables. However, when walking in the street, it will:

- make you look fat/pregnant
- rub against your skin and make you sweat/itch.

Many people therefore use them more as an open wallet, where you can wrap the straps around your hand (so that it can't be snatched) and then just carry it around by hand. This way you will get in the habit of carrying it with you at all times, or knowing exactly where it is and that it is safe at all times. It is also useful to have all your important documents in it, as they can be easily obtained whenever necessary from your daypack. They'll never get lost, and you know that you'll never leave them behind.

I do also carry a wallet with all my everyday bits and pieces in, such as cash, cards, ID, etc. I carry this in my pocket, and just walk along with my hands on it when I sense that there may be pick-pockets around in crowded areas.

Locals

- From all of this, you may now be worried that, wherever you go, locals are going to try and steal from you! This is certainly not the case, as there are not as many thieves around as you think.
- In a country where you don't know the people or the surroundings, you may tend to think that everyone is trying to rip you off. **However, this is just your natural 'survival instinct' making you paranoid to keep you alert.** This will tend to decrease the longer you travel.
- How I like to look at it is if you think of a foreigner in your home country walking down your high street... would your mum/dad/brother/sister rip them off? I hope not!

I can hear many of you thinking... 'well, maybe, Tom, but they won't be as visible as I would with a backpack and a map!'.

- For a start, when you go out to have a look around, you won't be wearing a backpack.
- Furthermore, you will quickly learn how not to stand out in a crowd.
- Therefore if you carry your things in a money belt, in your hand, you will be much less obvious than walking around with a huge stuffed 'bum bag' strapped to your lower regions!

Carrying money Top Tips

1. If you use a pocket, try and make sure that it has a button or a zip. No worries if it doesn't!
2. Back pockets = easy to pick, so get out of the habit if you do it.
3. Make sure that you air out your money belt/neck wallet every once in a while, as if it does get hot/sticky the contents can get a bit damp, and then everything will start to stink!
4. Avoid carrying all your money/credit cards in the same place. Split them up. Some in your daypack, some in your backpack, etc. This will minimise the risk of losing the whole lot.
5. Your daypack should be your most secure possession – your 'mobile safe' as it were. Always keeping it safe, or to hand, will ensure that you encounter no problems. At times when it is too bulky to carry around, take with you only the money belt (or whatever you choose to use) and don't let it out of your sight.
6. Good sense and awareness are not for sale in the shops!

Yes, there are thieves out there; it's a bad world. However, if you read your local paper, you will see that there are thieves on your doorstep. Have they affected you in a bad way?

The world of bad advice!

I feel that the worst problem here is that maybe too many people are talking to you at the moment about foreigners robbing you blind as soon as you step off the plane in a foreign country. It happened to me, and it'll happen to you. Once, while I was busking in Plymouth, a woman started talking to me about didgeridoos and Australia... advice for her son. I mentioned about this book and she started telling me about all the dangerous places on earth, and where she thought that her son should go. I asked her where she had actually been abroad. Answer: holidays in Europe! So why is she telling her son where he should or shouldn't go? Because like most of us she is scared, scared of everything unknown. She refused to believe me about how easy it is to travel in Australia, for example. I mean, why should I know... I've only done it!

Being safe

The point therefore is... if you are seriously worried about being safe, and carrying your things/money safely... DON'T BE! If you are reading this part of the book waiting for me to give you a foolproof way of never being robbed of your money, then I'm sorry. I can't/won't do that. The easiest form of protection for you and your valuables is simply being aware. As I said before, you are more likely to be robbed of your valuables in your home town than Kuala Lumpur. However, there is a whole section on safety in the book (see page 103), so have a read to hear some more thoughts on the subject. **My best advice if you are really worried about this is to stop listening to rubbishy advice from people who don't know what they are talking about!** They may think that they are helping you, but in the end they are just frightening you. You will be fine.

Hitch-hiking

R. L. Stevenson (1879)

Hitching is an 'art'

This is a unique subject on its own that is dying to have a whole book written about it. I would love to do it, as it is something that is very close to my heart; however, after writing this book I don't think I'll lift a pen ever again! Thirty years ago, so I've been told many a time, everyone would hitch-hike around. Young and old alike, picked up by 'ladies and gentlemen', and dropped off safely with a big smile, a hearty farewell, a piece of apple pie, and with thank you's all round. Those were the days, eh? Unfortunately, society changes, a few 'sickos' appear, and then hitching becomes a dirty word. 'You'll never be picked up!' 'You'll never get there!' 'You'll wait for hours you know!' And these comments are all from people who have hitched thousands of miles in their lives... erm, oh... sorry... you mean to say that they've never hitched in their life, and that they've never picked up a hitch-hiker! So that obviously gives them the authority to comment on hitch-hiking then! Stories, stories, stories. I've just got one word for it all... **BULL!**

I've hitched in Australia, all the way across Canada (alone), in France, and around the UK. Other friends of mine have hitched around Europe, all over Africa... **and all in the past few years**. 'Those were the days?' I'm sorry but, if you approach it correctly, **these are the days**. 'They're all long-haired wierdos with beards.' I have short hair, and always hitch clean shaven. 'They're all homeless.' Give me a break! 'If I pick one up, he'll kill me and rape my dog, or vice-versa. They're all dangerous, every one of them!' OK I'll be honest with you, I did squash a spider in the bath a few years back... but that was only because it was asking for it, as it refused to move when I asked it nicely! I think you get the message now. We live in a society where everyone is scared... to walk the streets, to be alone, to have doors unlocked.

Let's be serious for a moment

There is of course the serious issue which I must address. **Unfortunately with the way things are, and the way they will be in the future, society has stopped female hitch-hiking.** Many still do, of course, but I think that this is just inviting trouble. Please don't call me sexist when I say that **women shouldn't hitch unless with a companion**. I'm sorry but I've heard a lot of first-hand accounts of bad situations and it just seems that you would be taking too big a risk. Yes, it's true that I've heard a few bad accounts from men, but they sound a lot less frightening. You should also remember that there are other people involved here, i.e. your family. For them to know that you are hitching will be worry enough... but hitching alone! Well, I needn't say any more. You know your parents better than anyone else, so you'll know to what degree they won't sleep, and how much they'll worry.

Please, don't do it.

Why hitch-hike?

For a start it's cheap/free travel. If you do it right then you can normally travel to places just as quick, or even quicker than by bus or train. Quicker than by a plane... you're lying! When you have a series of long journeys to make, chatting to someone really does make the journey go a lot quicker. So why not talk to the person sitting next to you on the plane/train/bus? However, old grannies... beware, use only in desperation, and be ready for photos, irrelevant stories, and some totally remarkable connection to be made between the two of you (like her niece's friend living four doors away from your Auntie's chiropodist)... usually leads to the comment '... Tsk tsk... small world, eh?' At this point, bail out and head for the toilets, only reappear if she's gone/fallen asleep/passed away!

But the main thing for me is that you tend to meet some very interesting people, and some real characters. As I've mentioned before, most of what I call my 'real education' has come from lifts with a wide variety of people. How else can you meet the people of a country and get to understand what they are really like? After Canada, for example, I became clued up on all aspects of Canadian life. It is only when you learn to appreciate other countries and their people that you learn to appreciate your own.

I met people who were extremely happy with their lives, and others who hated their existence. **The thread seemed fairly similar all the way through... you've got to do what you enjoy in life, and do what you really want to do.** From what I witnessed this seemed to be the difference between success and mere 'existence'. But this is just my point of view, what I saw, and the beliefs which spur me on.

My theory was that if I could hitch across Canada I could do just about anything that I wanted in life, which included getting a good degree, writing this book, and getting a good job. The first two I've achieved, and I've since founded my own company... who wants to work for other people eh!?

So you think that you might like to hitch?

If you feel that you're the type of person who fancies the idea, or may even be in a situation where hitching seems the sensible solution, read on. Below I've given you a few rules which I always stick to, and they are proven in that they do work. However, as with a lot of things with this book... they're intended as a guide only please! Find your best method of hitching, stick to it, and you'll get better and better. **If you've never done it before, start off with a very easy distance and see how you get on.** Don't wait to be stuck out in the middle of nowhere with no confidence in yourself. Your body will tend to ooze confidence if it is there, making you as sharp as an infantryman's bayonet. If this gets picked up from 200 metres by a businessman in an Audi doing 80mph... you're on the right track! Depending on circumstances, if I don't get picked up in about 10 minutes, I ask myself... why not Tom? If you follow the basic rules and 'play the game', you should have no problems.

DO

1. **Be confident**, assertive, sure of yourself... look sharp, not spaced out.
2. **Have a sign** and hold it out where it can be seen. It should say where you are going in big bold letters and should always have a 'Please' in the native language on the bottom... remember you are politely asking for a lift, they have no need to give you one. For sign material you can't beat the side of a cardboard box.
3. Have your **backpack clearly visible**. Advertise 'I am a backpacker.'
4. Look **clean-shaven and tidy**. In hot countries only wear shorts, T-shirt, shoes and socks (if worn). This shows that you are hiding nothing, and that you really are as harmless as you look.
5. Have a **sign of where you are going next**, or your old sign of where you've been, next to your backpack or somewhere visible. This shows that you are not going to move in with them when you get to the destination, and that you are intending to move on somewhere else.
6. **Stand up straight**, don't crouch, as this is often perceived as a sign that you are hiding something. Smile, laugh, wave, make a show – *enjoy it*! Would you pick up someone looking miserable? No! The last thing you'd want is to try and cheer a hitch-hiker up. Someone else will pick them up. Game over, you lose!
7. **Stand in a place where people are going slow and can stop.** The only way you'll stop a car doing 80 mph is with a rocket launcher! Anyone doing 60 mph+ will see you, and then by the time they've decided to give you a ride, will be half a mile down the road, and unable to stop. Oh well, someone else will pick them up... not at that speed! You'll find that people are very selfish and won't skid or crash their cars just to pick you up! **The slip roads to motorways, at traffic lights (the last traffic lights out of town being the best), or just past a roundabout are always the best places.**

   A good tip is always to ask locals about where they think the best hitching spot is for you. If necessary, get a bus there. Quite often locals are happy to take you the couple a miles there to help you out. It shows you the true kindness of strangers and, anyway, it beats walking there!

   The position has got to be right. If there are traffic cones in the way, move them so people can pull over in safety. If they can't pull over, they won't. Last September I had to drive two miles back on myself to pick up two students hitching from a roundabout in Sheffield. They had been waiting for ages... because they couldn't be seen until you were right next to them, and with the cones it was extremely hazardous to pick them up. I only went back because I thought that they'd never be picked up (and because I'd just come back from Canada and wanted to do a good turn for them, like others had done to me). Point proved I hope.

8. **Be nice.** Many have decided at the last minute to pick me up after I have waved, smiled and said 'OK, no problem, thanks!' after they have said 'No'. If you say 'Well **** off then!' or have this written backwards on the back of your sign so that it can be read in the rear view mirror, you'll do yourself no favours, and give hitchers a bad name.

9. **Take a flag.** A British flag for example works wonders in Australia, Canada, America, and in a lot of parts of Europe, as well as other English-speaking countries of the world. They know that you're a 'real McCoy' backpacker, where you're from, and what language you speak. A lot of people are worried about having an awkward conversation/time with a person with a foreign language. Advertising really helps. If you are miles from home, present yourself properl, and show your nationality, ex-pats and British tourists will always pick you up. A good lift is a good lift!

10. **Have enough food and drink with you**, emphasis on liquids in hot countries. Also nice to offer to the driver, so they know they won't have to buy you food at any stops.

11. **Engage in interesting conversation.** This is a skill which you will learn that will always be useful to you. You don't need to be a chatterbox like me, just able to hold a conversation. The driver will then be more willing to take you where you want to go, and less willing to get rid of you at the first opportunity.

12. Carrying on from 11, **becoming 'friends' with the driver** always has the benefit of bonuses such as being offered food and a bed for the night. You may find work, have the chance to stay in a small community for a bit, anything like that. I have been invited to weddings, for Christmas, and always to 'visit again'. They are also welcome over here. It's amazing who you become friendly with!

13. **Check out the car as you approach it.** I turned down a lift in Canada because the driver said that he was going exactly where I wanted to go (a 10-hour drive) to visit his mum. But there was nothing, absolutely nothing, in the car... not even food and drink. Dodgy? Well, I thought so, so I turned him down. He was probably on the level, but I didn't want to take the chance. Children's toys/seats, or for that matter children, are usually a good sign of safety in a car. Businessmen tend to have suits, briefcases and work on the seats. General day-to-day items are also good

signs. You'll figure it out. However, only give the car a quick, subtle scan; if not they'll think that you're 'casing the vehicle'... and no lift buddy!

14. **Turn down lifts; don't be afraid to do it.** There will always be other ones (of course this doesn't apply to all situations!). If you don't like the situation, turn it down. If they're really OK they'll probably reassure you in some way. If they smell of alcohol... beware! Accidents do happen, and are more likely if the driver is drunk than not. And of course, the simple Golden Rule, **if you're going a long way, try not to take short rides**. It really won't help you if you hop along the motorway from junction to junction.

    This is why it is vital to write the best sign possible. Is the place too far to warrant putting it on the sign? Should you write two or three signs up and aim to get there in stages? Quite often it is useful to hold up the sign of where you want to go finally, e.g. Dover, on the bottom, and somewhere in between on top... London. Even better, put on motorways like M1, M25, RN1, on top, so people can see your route... more chance of a longer ride.

15. **Be prepared to give up and take a bus in remote areas** or if it gets late. Without a tent, the edge of the road is a nasty place to sleep at night. Even with a tent you are still vulnerable.

16. **Start as early as possible**, because everyone else does if they are going on long journeys. However, work out your times... is it rush hour traffic, i.e. are they going to work and no further?

17. **Plan your routes carefully**: foodstops, sleeping arrangements, etc.

18. **Would I pick me up?** If the answer is 'No', sort it out.

19. When you get a ride do **ask the person why they picked you up**. Don't ask this in any kind of menacing way or you're likely to get dropped off asap. But if asked nicely, hopefully you'll get a lot of the reasons 1–18, as this is solely what I have based my 'rules' on in the past.

20. When leaving the car, **leave the passenger door open** – to be closed last. Therefore if the person is a bit dodgy or simply forgets that your bag is in the back, they can't drive off leaving you with nothing.

There have always got to be a few 'Don'ts' lying around, right? OK, well here they are:

DON'T

1. **Wear a hat or sunglasses**, as people like to be able to see your eyes and your face. This can be a bit of a problem in hot, sunny countries if you need shade for your head, so adapt to suit your own needs. Personally, I will never wear either of these while hitching, as it is one of the main negatives people who have picked me up tell me about.

2. **Just stick your thumb out.** Genuine people will think... who is he, where is he going? They don't know. You'll wait a while if you try this one. Good luck to you!

3. **Go over the top trying to get a lift.** There is a difference between being funny and looking like an escapee from a nut house. You may also attract nutters.

4. **Stand for too long in direct sunlight** as you might well catch sunstroke. This has happened to me twice (something about not learning from your mistakes!). It is not very pleasant, and tends to ruin your day. This stems from me not wearing a hat. So do you or don't you? I can never really decide!

5. **Try and hitch through major cities.** They're very big, and unless your ride is going right through, you won't make it. A tip is to get out on the outskirts and take a bus in and out. If you want to bypass the city make sure you use the ring roads and get a ride that takes you all the way round. Cities? Avoid them like the plague/talkative old grannies.

6. **Hitch in dangerous places.** I know, seems obvious, but many tend to say 'Well it's only a short distance, so I'll risk it.' Fools... don't risk it!

7. **Hitch at night**, you're just asking for trouble.

8. **Get dropped off in the middle of nowhere.** Make sure that when you get in the vehicle you establish where the driver is going first. This will put the driver at ease as he/she will know that you really are safe, and that you are going somewhere. If you end up in the middle of nowhere, you'll find it very difficult to get picked up. People will naturally think that you've been thrown out of a car for some reason.

9. **Take offence.** There is always the odd comedian who will stop, wait for you to get close, and then drive off. Many of you may even have done it in the past. Well, having stitched your sides back up again, and dusted yourself off from where you have been rolling about on the ground in absolute hysterics, carry on hitching. If they were meant to be comedians they would have got jobs on the stage. This has never happened to me, but I have had the thumbs up from all members in the car, jokes and the odd comment. Unfortunately you laugh at them because
   - they're unoriginal
   - you can't hear a word because they've shouted out at 70 mph
   - you're never going to see them again in your life, so are you really bothered anyway?

My overall view on the subject.

You have a maximum of eight seconds to persuade a stranger that you are harmless enough, and so worth taking in their car. According to the rules above, by the time they pull over they will know:

- that you are a harmless backpacker
- that you are English, and speak English
- where you have been
- where you are heading for
- that you are hiding nothing
- that you are a friendly/funny person
- that you are clean
- that you are polite.

➤ By having a rough idea of the dos and don'ts you should have no problems.

As soon as you hear people saying, 'Well it's funny, because I've never picked up a hitch-hiker before!' then you know that you're on the right track. 'What goes around comes around!' I guess you probably knew that this expression was going to jump out again in this section, so I don't want to disappoint you! Most people who pick you up will have hitched themselves at some point. They will tend to look after you, feed you, give you a room for the night, and then take you to a good hitching spot in the morning. Why? Simply because somewhere down the line someone has done it for them, and in the future you will do it for someone else. It's true, I've already helped out a few young people hitching in the UK, something that I will always do, and in turn they will do the same for others.

For me, this is the best thing about it. If you can't afford to travel on your own money, you can travel on the kindness of strangers. There is a daft expression which says that, 'A stranger is just a friend that you haven't met.' Daft, but true? You will have a great time, and get up to all sorts of Shenanigans... like when I was completely led astray by a couple of 'mature' Canadian women, Nina and Tania, in the Rockies. I had a fantastic time, and now have two very good friends.

It can blow your mind!

Be warned, as it can be quite difficult at times, i.e. with conversation. People on long journeys will pick you up for conversation to make the time go quicker. Yes time does fly, especially if like me you are naturally chatty and have a lot to talk about. The problem, however, is when you do a number of hitches a day, which can be a bit of a head spin with the constant repetition of your life story, travels, etc. The conversations will always take the same course, and you'll find that you'll be able to repeat them over and over in your sleep. A good tip therefore is to have something major in the news to talk about. It will also be an education to find out what the average Frenchman thinks about nuclear testing, Australians about the British monarchy, and

Americans about anything not American (providing you explain it to them first!). Then go on the offensive and ask them questions about their life. No worries, eh?

A couple of words about trucks

If you can get rides in them then you are lucky, as they are spacious and comfortable on long journeys, but slow. However, you can have a laugh at all the truck stops talking to all the truckers and hearing what they have to say about life. Great greasy food as well. Diet, what diet! **Unfortunately in a lot of countries it is now becoming illegal for them to pick up hitch-hikers**, mainly for insurance purposes. Therefore they really won't as it means that they will lose their licences. So don't bank on getting their support. However (at the time of writing) it is still possible in the UK.

Where it is legal it is always worth a quick trip to any depots to see if there are any trucks going your way, and to see if one will give you a ride. Beware also if you're holding a big sign on the side of the road and a big truck roars past. The slip-stream that goes with it can knock you over, and also pull you into the inside lane… so when they go by… hold on to your pants!

Isn't it illegal to hitch in some countries?

Well, so I'm led to believe. However, I personally have had no problems. Generally the police will assess you, and if they feel that you, or anyone else, are not at risk, then they'll turn a blind eye. But I have heard from a number of friends that in some places any women caught hitching will be escorted back to the nearest town, or put on a bus. You see, **it's not me being sexist, it's the law** in many countries. Personally, I think that it is a great shame, but then if I had a daughter, I'm sure I would think a whole lot differently.

Is this for you?

Many would like to try it, but are not sure/confident enough to do so. If you are in this category, then why not try hitching a few small distances on an 'A road' nearby which goes from one town to another? For those of you familiar with the Essex–Suffolk border, many a time I have hitched from Stratford St Mary to Ipswich up the A12, or from Ipswich to Colchester on the A12, and then across to Mersea Island where my parents live. If you find it easy and enjoyable, then go for it. If not… well then you won't bother anyway! Hitching is very easy if done properly, and is very cheap. Like all things in life, practice makes perfect, and by the time you've done it a few times, you'll be a veritable master!

GOOD LUCK!

Chapter 12

Tips, hints and problems

❛ *"Old World charm" means "No Bathroom"!* ❜

Beware of dodgy advice

Adapters

Can be bought fairly cheaply. Get a multi-purpose worldwide one. They don't take up much space, and if you do find yourself carrying anything electrical, then you will be able to power it virtually anywhere. But, do you really need a hairdryer, iron, electric razor, or a portable beach BarBQ set?

Address cards

Carrying on from what I've just written above, a nice idea is to get some personalised name cards printed up, something which can be done virtually anywhere now. If there are a couple of you travelling together there is a great opportunity to get some humorous ones printed, guarantees that people don't forget you! They are also handy to put in the bottom of your bags, so that if your backpack does have the misfortune of getting lost by an airline or by other means, they will know your address and be able to get it back to you asap.

Addresses

You are going to meet, and make, some great friends. Not only that, you are going to meet a lot of them. Naturally you will take a decent address book. The only problem is that a few years down the line Mike Parkinson who used to live in Sudbury UK, will mean absolutely nothing to you, unless you have a very good memory or you keep in contact regularly. A good tip therefore is to note down where you are at the time, and certain characteristics. Mike, for example (who I haven't properly been in touch with since we were in Thailand three years ago...) looked uncannily like Russ Abbot. We happened to pick up on this wee fact... much to his disgust, and so 'Russ' was born. Hence 'Russ' is the name by which I remember who he is. This does seem a fairly obvious thing to do but, if you forget, and end up going to a country and decide to look up an address you have... bummer if you can't remember who it is, eh! Addresses are vital to get and keep hold of, especially of people that you got on well with, as the reunion parties and the odd 'long lost friend' kipping on your sofa 'on the way through the UK' is one of the bonuses of travel. It's great having friends dotted all over the world, and very useful too. Once you've got a few you'll feel like a real seasoned traveller, and dead popular too with Christmas cards from all over the world.

Airport taxes

Check for them at any time when you might be liable to have to pay them. Everyone always gets caught out by these taxes. At the very end of your stay in a country, none of the local currency left... never mind, cos you're getting on a plane to another country, so you'll be all right... get a bit of food on the plane, bit of sleep, time to... DOH! Airport Tax £20 payable before departure thank you very much we accept all major credit cards have a nice day! The hostels will normally be able to tell you how much it is, if there is one at all.

However, get in the habit of quickly asking at the airport when you arrive. Saves a lot of hassle!

Backpacks

Always practise packing, wearing and carrying it before you leave home, so you don't have to undergo major teething problems with it on your first days out while you are still trying to find your feet in a new country. You will get used to lumping it around very quickly, and find your techniques quick to master. Your backpack is your house/your secure item. Treat it with respect. If not, it will tire of you and deliberately fall apart. Get a good one... worth paying the money if you have to...

> NB: Never allow your pack to be searched by anyone who would come under the category of 'dodgy' in the dictionary, whether an official or not. It is too easy for them to slip something in and then start accusing you. Then all hell will let loose. All you have to do (as is your right) is keep hold of the bag and start unpacking it yourself. Don't make a big drama out of doing this, just calmly get on and do it... or you are likely to get nicked.

Bargaining

Look confident, have cash ready. The first price (in many less-developed countries) will be about three times the value of the goods, so you know roughly where you are going. But then you will have already have sussed out how much you are willing to pay for the item. The main thing to is enjoy it! It's all part of the travelling experience... and if you come away with what you consider to be a bargain, all the better. Don't be offended by any extraordinarily high prices, just realise that in many less-developed countries it is good business for salesmen to try and get the best price they can, and if they see a gullible tourist they will see if they can charge the earth for their goods. What might seem like not too much for us, may seem like a fortune to them. They will get to know pretty quickly that you aren't gullible, and will be quite happy to bargain a proper price. If not, then there is always another shop around the corner. Yes they may well chase you down the street trying to get a sale... and if they do, keep bargaining!

However, you must realise the difference between bargaining and just plain 'taking the piss'! If you are offered a handmade waistcoat for £10, and then you turn round and offer 10p, while accompanying the offer with a smug grin all over your face... they may well take offence. Don't be rude, be fair. Don't haggle over a matter of a few pence to you, as it really is bad manners! If you are in control, have the cash ready and treat it all like a bit of fun, you'll do well and become a bit of an expert within hours. Be serious and ready to walk away at a minute's notice, and you'll find you'll come back home with some real beauties as souvenirs. The only problem is that if your first stops are in these developing countries and you end up buying a few bits and pieces, they can be very bulky and so a real pain to carry around with you for the rest of your trip. You could think about sending them home (see Shipping/Posting items, page 172), but this can be risky. What can I say? Common sense I suppose. If it could break, and you've still got a long way to go... should you risk it? As for the bargaining... have fun!

Beaches

Great places to have a lot of fun at, but also a great place to break your neck. Sorry, but I'm not actually kidding on this one. I know of three blokes, all my age, who have run into the water and dived in, only to find that there is a sand bank there. It really isn't very nice, so be careful.

Other dangers are swimming in large surf if not used to it, and learning to surf for the first time. If, for the former, you are caught under big waves crashing down on you, don't panic, swim down deep, and let your body go limp every time the wave gets to you. Relax and let the wave take you. And then every time you see a break in the waves, go like **** for the shore! Learning to surf? Surfboards knock out English people... it is a proven fact! Until you get to the point where you can actually stand on it, make sure you have some sort of spectator there who can pull you out before you drown!

If when learning to surf you find a nice secluded beach with lovely little waves, and then get interrupted by local Aussies who keep shouting 'My Wave' at you... tell them to 'Bugger Off'!

Camping

Is definitely cheaper, and can be a really good laugh, depending on the area, time of year, seasons, wildlife, etc. Before going to a big campsite, find out if there will be anyone else there, as there is nothing worse than being the only tent in the middle of a massive national park... unless you like a bit of peace and quiet every once in a while. Check out for local holidays and festivals, as these are the times when the campsites will be full and lively. In Africa you can virtually stick your tent anywhere, but be careful to be safe as you could be very vulnerable, so try and stick to populated areas and campsites. Most developed countries have campsites with full amenities... where you can wash, use the BBQs, etc. Many, especially in Australia, will also have swimming pools and many hostels offer the opportunity to camp on their grounds for a smaller charge than the rooms. Camping is less secure, but as long as you have some way of securing the tent shut and don't keep your valuables in there, then you should have no problem. Most tents have holes on the zips so you can padlock it shut.

In areas with active wildlife such as bears, do heed the warnings such as not eating or leaving food in your tent. You often hear people saying that after a big night on the beers there is nothing worse than waking up next to someone you don't know. Well there is. Waking up with a hangover to find yourself face to face with a hungry seven-foot Grizzly is a point at which the shit really has hit the fan! It is a fact that in Australia a lot of tourists have been killed by crocodiles while posing in ankle deep water next to signs saying 'Beware Crocodiles'. Stupid? Well, I think so. But if you walk around with the attitude that you know it all and that everything everyone is trying to tell you is irrelevant, then you won't respect nature, and I'm afraid it won't respect you. Camping is cheap, fun, and a great way to meet more of the locals. In these situations you'll find an army of people willing to watch your tent for you, and always invitations for beer, dinner, etc. A great way to meet people and understand their way of life.

Cars

If you've ever bought a car in this country then you'll know what a risk it is. Just imagine the risks abroad, then, in a foreign country where it is obvious that you are a tourist, and where you are unlikely to be covered by any major insurances or helped by any local knowledge. Yet again, a lot of 'fors' and 'againsts' with this one. I know of many people who have found peaches... soft to touch, nice to look at, and sweet... a good deal. But on the other side of the bridge there are the lemons... hard and unpleasant, as they leave a bitter taste in your mouth. In this lottery, unless you know a lot about cars, it really will be down to luck and judgement. Cars bought in hostels can be good, as even though they have been around the clock 10 times and have more spare parts than the Halford's Christmas collection, you know that it does actually run and that it will get you across America if you pray hard enough. The backpackers that are selling it, although anxious to get a sale, will at least tell you what they have replaced and how much they have had to spend on it. They will also tell you all you need to know about how much it will cost you in petrol, insurance, tax, etc. However, once you've taken it for a spin round the block they won't tell you that: a) if you go over 55mph it blows up; b) there are more than two fairly lightweight people in it then the back tyre will come away; c) they've been trying to sell it for five months, but everyone apart from you has thought that it is the biggest pile of crap since the 1998 England World Cup campaign, and that they have all gone away in fits of laughter!

But remember that if you do buy a second-hand car, there really isn't too much that you can do about it if you have bought a lemon and you know that the bloke who sold it to you knows this. Just make sure that you are insured, and if possible check if any existing cover, e.g. the AA will cover you overseas. I know for example that the AA can cover you in America if you have certain policies... so do check.

The other thing to look out for is unscrupulous, dodgy-looking blokes... you know the sort I'm talking about. Many have been known to advertise their cars on the hostel notice boards, and so are naturally thought to be travellers themselves. These con men will be very good, and will have the most believable stories ready for you. They will check that you are about to drive off miles away, so that when the car does eventually go 'pop!', you'll be so far away that there is nothing you can do about it.

1. Why not find a local mechanic, slip him a few notes and see if he will have a look at any cars that you are thinking of buying... a few pounds now may save you a lot of money later on.

2. Ask at the hostel you are staying at... what do they suggest about buying cars in that area/country?

3. If you know that you are going to go to a country with the idea of definitely buying a car and travelling around for a while, why not get to know a few of the basics over here first?

4. Embassies have been known sometimes to have a few cars... always worth a try.

5. Take time to shop around. Don't expect a Rolls-Royce, but don't accept a half-loaded skip. You need something reliable. If it looks good, all the better, but your fellow backpackers won't really care.

6. If you buy common makes, then you'll always be able to get parts and they'll probably be cheaper. However, having to wait for specialist parts for your 'Studmobile Mustang peachofacar awsomepower looksfantasticbaby GTi Turbo spoilers wings theworks luckyifikeepitontheground tossers car'... then I'll be the first to laugh at you!

7. When buying, pretend that you are hanging around for a while, get their address so that you can 'call round' if you have any problems. This should help you with the odd 'blagger'.

8. Remember you have to sell it. So allow yourself time, and give yourself a chance, by selling it in a major backpacking area where there is a demand for cars, places like Sydney, New York, etc. Advertise as much as you can, and be prepared to negotiate well. You probably won't regain all the money

that you spent, but do try, as the buyers may be very keen to buy and get going. Think about what you wanted to hear when you were buying, and tell it to them. However, if you have a deadline for when you must leave the country, make sure you have plenty of time to sell. If not, you may end up flogging it off for peanuts, which will really annoy you!

9. Hot countries, old cars may have problems with the air-conditioning system packing up. This can affect other parts of the car and can end up being very costly.

Always pretend like you have an idea about what you are looking at. Learn a few questions to ask. Be confident. You are less likely to be ripped off. Good luck!

Changing your plans?

Make sure you let someone know. By keeping in regular contact with people this will cause no problems. However, if you are expected in one place, but are 'largeing it up' somewhere else, then you may cause others needless anxiety.

Chill out!

Stepping off an aeroplane onto the hot tarmac of an unfamiliar country, an unfamiliar language, and what seems like a multitude of gabbling people, all running around, eyeing you up, etc., can be daunting. This kind of situation can scare the pants off anybody, whether 18, just out of school, and just landed in the first country, or 24, a graduate, and a seasoned traveller. Whether it is Sydney, Delhi, Marrakech or Mexico City, it will always seem overwhelming and possibly too much to handle. The secret is not to walk to the other end of the airport and book yourself on the first plane back home, but... to chill out. Take a deep breath, and remember that you are there to enjoy yourself, and that you have all the time in the world.

The best thing to do is find your way to the hotel/hostel/campsite/etc., dump all your things (ensure they are safe – if unsure, take all the important bits with you) and then go 'walkabout'. Have a wander. For your first wander, relax and have a little look at everything in your surroundings. Avoid looking at maps and guidebooks, as this does tend to advertise yourself as a tourist and may make you look a bit vulnerable. Just place your things in a normal white plastic bag, and wander around without bringing attention to yourself. Take in the surroundings, and you'll soon get used to the sound of the language, the smells, the way of life, etc. If people do come up and talk to you, ask yourself why. Don't get lost, be wary of where you walk, and have the name and address of where you are staying written down on a piece of paper, so that you'll always be able to find your way back.

When you get back, I always find that getting a few beers inside you tends to help. After a few everything seems a lot easier, slower and less overwhelming. A few more on top of that and suddenly everything seems easy, friendly and familiar. Even more, and then (for me) all the women turn into famous supermodels, and they're all in love with me. And then I normally wake up with a stinking hangover. Well there's a little bit more about me that you didn't really need to know... but what the hell!

Courier flights

At the very time of writing I am actually on one of these courier flights, using it for my own needs, but also as a bit of a 'road test' for this book. This is a fantastically cheap way to travel, but is relatively unknown. How it works is that certain airlines (British Airways for example) have a system where they can make you a courier for the day. When boarding the plane you will be given a set of documents which you will in turn hand to someone to put in the plane's safe. Once you get onto the other side, you pick up the documents and hand them to someone else as soon as you get off the plane. The documents are all business documents, and so fully security checked. You are required to be 18+ and to wear smart clothes. You get the usual baggage allowance and the ticket is non-refundable. The only drawback is that you have to set a date to return by, and you are normally bound to a maximum of one or two weeks depending on where you go to. However, it is extremely cheap, quite often cheaper than a one-way ticket if you are going to buy one of those anyway. But be warned, it is a very popular way to travel, as it is so cheap. Flights go every day, and so if you put your name forward early you can just about go whatever day you want to. If you are after a cheeky cheap trip for a couple of weeks, always try the end of the month where the fares are reduced on flights not sold. At the time of writing flights are available for: New York, £130 return; Bangkok £250 return; Buenos Airies £200 return, all of which include insurance!

For more information write to:

British Airways Travel Shop
Room E328, 3rd Floor, E Block
Cranebank, S551
Heathrow Airport
Hounslow
Middlesex TW6 2JA

Tel: 0870 606 1133; lines may be busy due to popularity, but keep trying.

Creases in your clothes?

Just at the point where you don't have an iron and you are out to impress? Well, no more! Simply get hold of a few pairs of old tights. Then pull the item of clothing up into the tights. You will be left with a big sausage shaped thing that you can simply coil into your bag. When you take the garment out... hey presto, no creases!

Credit cards

Always useful to have in emergency situations, as they are an invaluable source of 'large amount of money quick'. They are also handy for their insurance purposes, and very useful for providing emergency aid to distant countries when needed. Remember the Barclaycard advert with Rowan Atkinson with the guy with the leg infection 'You're looking for his Barclaycard Bof? This is no time to go shopping! No... I'm going to have to locate the wound and suck the poison out myself!' In the end the bloke is airlifted out. When I met Amanda Fogg in Indonesia, she told us about her friend who, while in India, had some sort of stomach upset, and so 'blocked it up' with Lomotil. This is usually a good idea, but in this case she must have blocked the infection in, and so it festered and got worse. The result was that she was desperately ill, and Amanda feared for her life. In desperation she rang one of the credit card companies on their emergency number. Within 24 hours she had been flown back to a hospital in England. She recovered. A true story, and one which I always use to remember to keep those emergency numbers safe. Because, at the end of the day, if there is an emergency and you need help, these boys will move mountains. (A quality insurance cover will also do the same for you, so a quick reminder following this story for you to get decent insurance!)

Beware... as in some of the poorer countries of the world they are very good at making fakes. There have been occasions where numbers have been taken, signatures forged, and extra zeros added. You will only find out about this when you eventually get home, and there really isn't much that you can do about it. So, to be sure, make sure that you take the carbon copies (which you are entitled to do), and in cases where you are not sure about the credibility of the shopkeeper, don't hand your card over until you have at least three character references, a certificate of reliability from their government, and proof that the bloke does in fact own the shop that you are standing in! If in doubt, try and pay by other means.

Cultural practices

One of the biggest problems that young travellers have is accidentally offending the locals. I can honestly say that I've never met a traveller who has gone out of their way to offend the locals of the countries they visit, most being very respectful of their hosts. However, I have been present when some travellers have offended someone in the street due to pure ignorance – girls not covering up in certain countries, accidentally forgetting when it gets a bit hot; a few lads forgetting to stick on a sarong when going into a temple; wearing leather sandals in a Hindu temple (cows are sacred); and, a classic among the relaxed backpacker community, sticking your feet up on the table, the seat or out of the side of a hammock when in ultra-relaxation mode and so showing the soles of your feet to passers-by – this, in quite a few Asian countries and other cultures around the world, is seen as very offensive as it represents the lowest part of your body (imagine someone getting their bare botty out in front of your gran in a public place... that kinda stuff!).

It is important therefore to do a bit of research. As there are so many cultural practices that vary from country to country, I'm not going to go into them all here. This is something that should be a serious, but fun, part of your travel preparation. Before you go to a country do some homework. The best place to swot up is in the guides books. Rough Guides, Lonely Planet, Footprint, etc. all have fantastic sections in each of their country-specific books – just look in the index for 'Etiquette'. Alternatively there is a 'Guide to etiquette on gapyear.com' that sums all this up for you.

Things to learn about and look out for:
1. **Religious festivals, holidays and daily customs/routines.** Festivals and holidays are key here. Find out when they are and if you are going to turn up bang slap in the middle of one. Ramadan is one of the most famous ones – during this time when the local Muslims are fasting it is offensive for you to eat and drink in the street. This happens at different times around the world. While you are doing your research try to learn a little bit about the history of the festival, what it is all about and maybe take the time to learn something about the religion, the people and the surrounding culture – you'll thank me for saying this one day when you are able to answer one of the hard-ass questions on 'Who wants to be a Millionaire?'!

   Daily customs and routines are worth noting, especially if you accidentally interfere in something that you think is a great spectator event – you won't be popular. They may look cute in their colourful dress with their flowers and their singing in the street, but your flashing camera, grins and inappropriate behaviour may not be welcomed if they are mourning their dead or honouring their ancestors – imagine a random stranger popping up and taking photos of your relative's funeral. Get the point?

2. **Behaviour on the street while you are mooching around.** Try to take a photo of someone in the street where they believe that this takes your spirit away and your camera will be sent to Smashville! Also, it is generally considered rude (by most people) to take snapshots of strangers, especially if you are in a country where your weekly wage at Kentucky McDogburger is equivalent to a family's annual budget – i.e. are they just there to

entertain you on your trip? No? Then ask permission (which does ruin the natural shot I know). Why not sit down with them for a bit and try to communicate and get some natural shots then? Wow, what a thought – heading round the world and actually learning something from the people you rush by daily!

Surely the only way to develop your own cultural understanding and deal with culture shock is to open your eyes to what is going on in front of you and let a bit of someone else's culture in... no? Haggling: there is a point when you cross the 'I'm taking the piss' line. Drinking alcohol in countries where it is frowned upon: there is a point when you cross the 'I'm taking the piss' line. Visiting temples, public places, shrines etc.: there is a point when you cross the 'I'm taking the piss' line. Get the idea?! Remember, you are a visitor to their country. Everyone has a story about ignorant tourists in their own country. Take note, this could be you – so know where the line is and respect it... then the locals will respect you. Simple as that!

3. **Meeting people and communicating**. As you are probably aware we live in a fairly developed world where Fairy Liquid makes your hands 'oooh so soft', and Andrex produce poo tickets that make the end of a good 'sit-down' a pleasurable, sometimes prolonged, experience (well, for me anyway... high-fibre diet and all that!). Michael Palin's foreword to this book even suggests that he approves of Bloomsbury's choice of paper for the pages for the very same reason (an enduring image). However, in many less-developed countries it is still the norm to use hole-in-the-floor toilets and your left hand to, ermmm...wipe! Crude I know, but there is a serious point here. As a result of its daily task, the left hand is not used for eating food, accepting food/things, shaking hands etc. A huge cultural 'no-no' in many Muslim and Hindu countries and generally in countries where you are aware of similar toilet habits.

In cultures based around respect (unfortunately I do not class our own as this), do you best to show it. Be humble, respectful, polite and understanding of your hosts. Yup – this means that you may have to try food that you don't want to eat but remember – it ain't gonna kill you and it may be disrespectful to your hosts to refuse it; they may have spent a long time preparing it or indeed spent a lot of their weekly budget buying it. In our culture it is certainly polite to have a 'ladies first' attitude, but don't try and push this in a country with a 'men first' culture. Why? Imagine a visitor to your home (with a 'men first' culture) helping themselves to stuff before your mum, your sister or your gran (you know the score – grabbing the few wee crispy spuds that you know your mum likes – and she cooked the damn meal!).

The secret? Take time to check out every new situation. Scope the room out, see what people do and if you don't know... ask! Everyone will understand that cultures are different and they will certainly appreciate the fact that you have asked and are making an effort. Pointing, burping, passing wind, eating with your mouth open/closed, washing your hands before dinner/during dinner/after dinner, removing your shoes, the way you sit, the way you look at people, how you accept things, whether to accept things, facial hair, body hair (boys and girls!), bare shoulders, the way you meet people, the way you leave people, who eats first, who eats last, when people don't eat, when people don't drink (alcohol) blah blah blah blah blah...! All things you need to be aware of.

OK – I can feel a bit of panic coming on. Be cool, don't worry. Do your homework before you go (go to the library and read those guide books or head onto gapyear.com) and just do what comes naturally. Remember to open your eyes when in any situation overseas and check out what is going on and what is the norm. If you are faced with something you are unfamiliar or uncomfortable with, remember... that is why you are travelling... to learn all this stuff. So, if your host in Mijanikstan (just made it up – doesn't really exist) smiles after his meal, winks at his wife, raises his hand and deliberately cracks off a good 'un, don't be too shocked! Merely point out that this was unusual and never seen back home. When they state that in Mijanikstan it is the most respectful thing you can do to show your approval to the cook, simply suck in your shame, hide your embarrassment, tuck your dignity into your pants, grit your teeth, part your cheeks, wink at the wife... and let rip!

Travel... broadens the mind! Let it.

Dehydration
Very easy to get dehydrated, but easily avoided by constant drinking. Ensure when buying bottled water that there is a good seal on the bottle, and that it hasn't been tampered with. A lot of money can be made by filling old bottles up with bad water and then selling it as the good stuff! However, if you do get dehydrated, just drink plenty of water mixed with salt and sugar. Then take a rest. You should be restored in no time. If you find yourself getting dehydrated regularly, you may find that you have some diabetic tendencies. This does not mean that you are a diabetic (unless you are of course!), but you should be aware that you might well be prone to headaches, dizziness, etc. if you don't get enough liquid. Note – the moment you feel thirsty, you are dehydrated, so keep hydrated by constantly sipping water when hot.

Didgeridoo

A classic Australian instrument whose sweet rhythmic sounds are played by me on the streets of the UK for the entertainment of the public! Note real spelling is 'dijeridu', but no one recognises it! [Useless fact No. 8356]

Diet

Watching your diet is the point of this little Tiperoony. It is very easy to live off fast food when you are travelling... burgers, chips, hot dogs. In a few of the Asian countries it is easy/safe to go with what you know best... Pizza! All very well, but when you are travelling it really is essential to think about what you eat, and to make sure that your body does get what it needs.

Fruit is good for you and cheap. This is from someone who never used to eat any fruit. I now make sure that I do eat an orange or an apple a day. However, when buying fruit off the street, don't eat it straight away, take the skin off and make sure that the skin is not pierced. Oranges therefore are safe, as well as giving you a good balance of Vitamin C. Granola bars/muesli bars – again you are looking at someone who looked at these on the shelf and then picked up the Mars bar next to it. Believe it or not they don't actually taste like they look – sawdust! – but are actually very tasty. These chewy/crunchy fruit and oat bars are good for you and will give you much-needed energy for walking around a lot. Bananas are again very good for you, and are often a lot tastier and bigger than the ones that you get over here. Porridge/oats are again cheap and good for you. The sachets are easy to store, there are lots of different flavours, and all you have to do is add water. It is one of those foods that 'sticks to your ribs' in the morning and sets you up for the day.

Do bear in mind that I am not someone who eats like a sparrow. In fact I do eat like the proverbial 'pig'... I'm not shy when it comes to food! If you are like me you might find it a bit of a hassle/expense to fill those hollow legs. However, rice, pasta and bread are the easy options. Carbohydrate city! If you have an appetite like that, then you'll probably burn it all off anyway. The only thing is that you may have to learn a few little culinary skills; it's simple enough to make that pile of rice/pasta taste anything but dull.

If you can't cook, it's about time that you did learn a few of the basics now. You'll find that if you are staying at a particular hostel for a week or so, and if they do have kitchens with fridges, cookers, cutlery, etc. (as most do), then it is cheaper to do a shop at the beginning of the week which will last you for the week. You can then get into the habit of cooking yourself a good, decent meal everyday. This will be a lot cheaper and healthier than buying food from the shops or take-out each day. This also turns out a lot cheaper if you are travelling with others and you agree to share the cost of the food. Cooking and eating together will then take away the pain of being in a kitchen, if it is as appealing to you as swallowing the contents of Bernard Manning's dirty underwear drawer!

Drugs

If it is in your nature to delve a little in these murky waters, make sure you take the highest precaution. In most of the countries that you visit, drugs will be a lot cheaper than you are used to and in much more abundant and open supply. Being a traveller in some places will mean that you will be offered them left, right and centre. This is what your parents fear, and in certain places, they are right. However, if you are not into drugs it is easy to say no and be left alone. Despite what your parents or other 'wise' people have told you, you will not be chased or harassed until you buy some. These people know that there will probably be someone who will buy round the corner, and anyway they won't want to draw attention to themselves. If you do intend to buy, take the following advice:

- In some countries there is still the death penalty for being involved with drugs.
- You really don't know what you are getting. The drug may be different from what you normally get at home. This could be lethal to you, or do you untold damage.
- It is not unknown for corrupt officials or bloody good con men to sell you something and then threaten to have you arrested. If you are young, out in Africa/Asia/South America, and face the possibility of a long jail sentence, or possibly even the death penalty, you will pay anything they ask for! In this position you will be blackmailed/robbed of thousands of pounds.
- In situations such as the above, don't try and fight it. You have been caught out, and you will have to learn by it and pay financially for the consequences. If they are corrupt enough to actively go out to get you, they will be corrupt enough to see that you suffer if you don't play by their rules. Always pay the price, and get out asap. And then, most importantly, learn by it.
- Heard stories of drugs being dropped in drinks?... If it happens here in the UK, why not on the other side of the world? It has happened to people I know, so to prevent it get in the habit of holding/carrying your drink with your hand over it. If you put up some form of protection, it won't be tried... they will only try anything like this if it is easy and guaranteed to work.
- Drug smuggling. Well if you try this then you're a bigger pillock than I think you realise. I suggest you have a sit down and have a really good think about your life.

There have been cases of drugs being put into unsuspecting people's bags so that they can be smuggled across the border. Very rare, and easily avoided by keeping a very good eye on all your belongings all the time. You will invariably be with others on a border crossing, and so you are unlikely to be chosen as they have to somehow get the drugs back on the other side. You are no good because they won't be able to get to you or the bag without being seen. Very unlikely then.

> NB: All of the above are either very unlikely, or can easily be avoided by your own actions. I am not trying to fuel the paranoia of worried parents, or your own fears generated by various programmes or articles that you may have read. I am a great believer in the idea that if you are aware of these things, then you will be able to face up to them and deal with them. It will also be no shock to you if you go to a place like Bali and in the middle of the street an Indonesian slides up to you and whispers 'Mushrrrooms... mushrrrrrooms... you want to flyyyy to the moon tonight... !' 'Eeeeerm... nno thank you very mmuch, we're just off down to the beach... But I'm sure the moon's very nice this time of year... see ya!' as you hurry away. No problem, dealt with.

So please don't worry, just be aware. I've been offered drugs in Manchester and even on the streets of lowly old Ipswich. It happens, it's a part of life. Just as long as you know to watch your luggage at border crossings and after you have packed to leave the country. Also to be suspicious of anyone taking an unnecessary interest in your flight details, home address, etc. before you leave. If you do buy from someone on the street, check that what you have is what you paid for, and that the person selling it isn't an undercover police officer, or a con man who when offering you 'grass', really does mean... grass! Just be cool about it all, eh?

Eggs

How do you know if they are OK to eat? Why... roll them of course! If they are a bit dodgy they will roll OK. If they are good to eat, then they will not roll properly and wobble all over the place (as the yolk moves around). Also bad eggs float in water; good eggs sink... others hatch and, as such, make a poor omelette.

Embassies

Can't bail you out, but will always be there to advise you and get you any help that you need. Any problems, don't be afraid to go to the Embassy, or to get in touch with them. (See '**Health and emergencies**'.)

Expensive hotels

Have good toilet facilities if the ones that you are exposed to just will not do. A special mention must go to Raffles Hotel in Singapore which in my opinion has a five-star set of dunnies and, for the lads, self-flushing urinals as soon as you take a step back! What else could a man (or woman) want?

Flights

I used to enjoy flying, but after a string of flights the novelty soon wore off and the whole shebang of airports, planes and flying lost its appeal.

Tips are:

- Ask for it! If you prefer a window or aisle seat, ask for it. Similarly with vegetarian or vegan meals.
- On long flights, always find out if it is a full flight. If empty, see if you can get one of the middle seats so that you have plenty of room and can stretch out over the four seats when you want to sleep. In those situations all you are going to see from the window are the clouds and, anyway, when you land, you can probably jump into a free window seat to see the view as you come in.
- If you like to watch the films, ensure that your seat is not too close/too far away from the screen. Ask at the check-in. Be nice and polite and you'll find they are extremely helpful. Getting a good seat in the right position can make or break a flight.
- As you are booking in advance always check the arrival time of when you land, as the last thing that you need is to fly in to somewhere in the middle of the night with no accommodation and no knowledge of where to go.
- Big flights always have food wastage with people not eating meals etc. If you are hungry, being nice and polite to the stewards/esses normally brings you the benefit of a second or even a third meal (I even had a fourth one time... good old Quantas – well I was fairly hungry at the time!) Backpackers are often seen as easier passengers for the airline staff – rarely complaining, and grateful for what they get. Furthermore, they are more relaxed travellers, and so are usually pleasant and interesting to talk to. Getting to know your steward/ess on long flights makes your flight, and their job a lot better. On the flight into Australia we were fed beer after beer, extra portions, the works. It was one of the best flights that I have ever had.
- Overbooked flights: two fantastic words that you can take full advantage of as a backpacker. As you have all the time in the world, when you hear that the flight is overbooked go immediately to the flight operator and offer your seat up. You will become their best friend as it helps them out, but you will also do yourself a massive favour as you will be fully

compensated. To give you an idea, you could get as much as a night in a five-star hotel, cash bonuses, meals, free upgrades, etc. I just missed out on one when I came back from Canada and I was absolutely gutted! If you get one, don't tell me about it as I'll probably throw up!

- If you are pleasant/charming to the check-in employee, look smart and clean and ask really nicely, they may well give you a free upgrade into business class. Again I have known this to happen but, despite asking thousands of times, I have got absolutely Jack... and I can be a real charmer when I want to at times (although I'm not admitting that, I'm just using it to illustrate a point!).

- Waiting at airports. Again, try and chill out about it. Remember that you have all the time in the world. So the plane is delayed – big deal, who cares... you shouldn't. Just ensure that in your day bag you have everything that you need to keep yourself occupied. You'll probably find yourself among a group of backpackers so you'll all join up, start chatting, and then the time will fly anyway. You can also use these moments as an excuse to go up to people (especially if travelling alone) and make a few friends... Some may be going to the same place as you at the other end, so you'll discuss plans, taxi shares, etc.

Food

Beware, as in all countries the food will be prepared in ways that you may not be used to. If you struggle through a meal drinking copious amounts of water and then devouring four ice creams at the end... and in the morning while on the toilet your backside goes down for a drink... you will realise that it was in fact red chilli, and not tomato, that you were eating!

Gifts

It may be illegal to bring certain gifts and souvenirs back in to the UK, or to take them out of the country – so do try and find out the score before you buy a seven-foot python and lug it all the way round Asia only to find the guy at Heathrow taking it off you... it'll only piss you off!

Guidebooks

Like this one should be treated as 'guide only'. Unfortunately people tend to treat the guidebooks as bibles, trusting every word and doing everything literally 'by the book'. Yes it may well be the 'best madras in the world' in the restaurant four doors away from the main youth hostel in Kuala Lumpur, but if you find that the restaurant is packed with backpackers all sweating over a madras, and reading the same book... !

Hello! Have you seen all the other empty restaurants down the road with similarly good (and probably cheaper) menus? Probably just as good. Try not to walk around with your head down ticking off all the places in the guidebooks. You have spent a lot of money to come a long way. By all means use the guidebooks for reference, but remember to look up and take everything else in as well. Usually locals, people who work in the hostels and other backpackers can give you better advice about what to see when you're out there… so always ask and always remember to write EVERYTHING down, as it may be extremely useful later on down the road.

Gung ho travellers

These boys (and girls of course) are usually recognised by the crazy nicknames they have, and the bull-shit advice that they give. Yes you may think that 'Pyscho Jim' and Adrenalin 'Junkieman' Dave are a great laugh and have got a lot of stories to tell in the bar… but would you share a room with them without checking their names against those on Interpol's 'Most Wanted' list first? These are the guys that will drink and drive, go where they really shouldn't, and will say they have been where they really haven't. They won't be around when you decide to engage in some of the local customs they have bragged about, or gone surfing in shark-infested waters with the knowledge that all it takes is 'one hard smack on the nose and the big woosy shark will run away with tears in its eyes'… it won't! The moral of this? Do take the advice you are given by other travellers with a massive pint of salt.

Hairdressers

Can you cut hair? Do you own some clippers? If so, here's an idea for you. On the 'backpacking circuit' there are always those who put adverts up for haircuts. If you have hair like mine that goes afro (Michael Jackson aged 5 – that's me after six weeks without a haircut!), it needs to be cut… and this can be expensive. By doing the odd haircut here and there you will:

- earn your rent for the night or even longer
- keep yourself fed for a week if you do loads
- get yourself known and find it easy to make friends
- become very popular
- get a lot of free beeer!

Just remember to put up a notice on the hostel notice board wherever you stay, stating where you are, how long you'll be there, and the price. If you keep it cheap, you'll always find plenty of business.

Injections

When you go to your doctor for your check-up, make sure that it is done a good few months before you go so that you have plenty of time for them to stick loads of needles in you. If, like me, the thought of injections and needles sounds as appealing as having an umbrella opened up in your bottom, don't worry. It doesn't actually hurt that much, the worst will be like a bee sting at the most. Turn away, close your eyes and grit your teeth... or if you think you're hard... ask them if you can do it yourself! The doctors will be able to tell you which injections you will need, and you do need them, so go and get them done, and then keep photocopied evidence of them.

Insurance
You need to take insurance. If you haven't read the section on it head there right now – page 65.

Jobs/working abroad
Make sure that you have all the necessary visas if you want to work in any of the countries that you are going to visit. The most popular is the Working Holiday Visa for Australia, which you can get on the spot from the Embassy in London (see Appendix 3 at the back of this book).

Australian Working Holiday Visas
If you are going to Australia on a working holiday, you will need a visa. The application forms sent out via Consyl Publishing's offices are accompanied by a copy of the publication 'Travel Australia'.

All you need to do to receive the forms is to send an A4 (approx. 12 inches x 9 inches) self-addressed envelope with four loose first-class stamps (UK only). Include with this a short note stating you would like Working Holiday Visa application (form 1150).

The address to send your request to is:

Australian Outlook
3 Buckhurst Road
Bexhill-on-Sea
East Sussex
TN40 1QF
www.consylpublishing.co.uk

Within two days of receiving your request for forms they will have them in the post and on their way back to you.

Working in Australia
If you decide to work in Australia, make sure you apply for a 'Tax File Number' as soon as you can, as you'll need it if you get work which is taxed... or don't bother and get taxed at a rate of about 50 per cent... it's up to you! Remember all your photocopies of any educational qualifications that you may have. This

visual proof may be the difference between you being given the job or told to ring back in a couple of weeks. A driving licence is sometimes essential to have. You see, the thing about backpacker work is that if you really want it, and you look around... you'll find it. Employers are always looking to take backpackers on because quite often there is a bit of work that takes about a week/fortnight to do. So they will be quite happy to take you on because they know that you might only want a couple of weeks' work before you move on. Cash in hand, no working visas needed, and you'll be long gone. Perfect!

However, do be aware of backpacker exploitation. This can happen in 'picking' farms such as those for bananas, mangoes, pineapples, etc. It is hard work, it can be an experience, and it can be very well paid. But before you get taken out to the back of beyond and so are at the owner's mercy (as you get taken miles out of town and so are stranded if you don't want the job) find out exactly what you have to do to earn the money, what they might expect you to pay them, and how much money you will realistically be left with at the end of the week. Why? Because many are offered a lot of money to go and pick fruit, and then find out that they are charged a ridiculous amount for food and accommodation, transport, a picking licence, special picking shoes, owner's holiday, daughter's car, etc. However, don't be put off by this. If you ask the

... steaming as well...

questions first then the honest farmers will make themselves clear to you... dishonest ones will tell you to clear off, as you will probably put gullible backpackers off. With the honest ones if you put the hard graft in you can earn a lot of money.

Unless desperate try to find work that you enjoy; don't be forced into work you don't like purely for the sake of working. Look around for jobs, and don't be afraid to do a bit of bargaining with the employer... remember that you 'don't actually exist' in the countries you visit (make of that what you will!). BUT... also remember that working without a visa is illegal and you can be deported for it. There have been recent reports from Australia that officials are doing spot checks on farms and other workplaces and arresting and deporting all those without visas. By the way, if you get deported you have to pay the costs of deportation, which may be substantial... and you also get banned from going to that country ever again. Yes, people do work illegally, but understand the consequences if you get caught.

If you are confident enough, go out and look for work, ask everywhere you go, i.e. offer to do work in the hostels in exchange for food and accommodation... in fact in Australia, for example, many hostels do this anyway. Good luck!

Keeping in touch
See the chapter '**Parents**'.

'Kind people'
May offer you food or drink. Why? Make sure you are aware of their intentions, as mugging people while under the influence of drugs has been known to happen in some countries, and 'date rape' is also something girls should all be aware of. Again, I don't want to alarm you, but if you are aware of these things then they are less likely to happen. However, the sixth sense that you will develop will allow you to distinguish between these and the genuine offers. Sometimes it is a good idea not to spurn offers as it may well cause offence. In these situations an exchange of gifts is a great idea and may well get you a long way... so those balloons, pens, English postcards I've mentioned under '**Packing**' may be a good idea after all!

Languages
Learning key phrases I've found to be a great way of getting what you want. Starting off in their language unless fluent gets you nowhere, as you are left staring at them like a perplexed pike as they jabber on at you in gobbledegook as the only phrase you know translated means 'Good morning sir/madam, and how are you this morning?'... and then they tell you! Bad move. Start the conversation in your broken 'Tourist speaks English to local but with a fake French accent'... to establish the ground rules – and then throw in the odd bit

Chat-up lines in virtually every language under the sun (especially Swedish) can come in very handy, but then that's a different story altogether!

of badly pronounced Thai for 'How much is it?' normally said with my cheeky grin and a little smile. This is always appreciated, and gets you a long way. Never get the local to write down the words for you, always write in your diary how it sounds to you, e.g. 'Nissan bulla'... which is 'Good morning, how are you?' in Fijian... a very polite thing for you to say to a Fijian, and they love it! Easy to remember... the new 4x4 from Nissan, the Nissan bulla!

Late arrivals

Make sure you pre-book a bed in advance. If you book your hotel/hostel well in advance you can just exit the airport, head to the nearest taxi and say 'Hotel Bodeglas, Mr Taxi Driver'. It may be good or bad, but at least it will be a safe bed for the night and will save you the hassle of faffing around late at night in unfamiliar territory. You can then sort yourself out in the morning.

Litter

If this is a bad habit of yours, please get out of it, and don't drop litter in places such as Ayers Rock, the Taj Mahal, the Himalayas, or in my street/house/bedroom. It's a disgusting habit, you're lazy, no more said.

Locals

I have mentioned locals throughout the book. Maybe I should label this under 'culture shock', because I feel that this is the main problem that causes the concern and anxiety when faced with 'locals' for the first few times. The main tips are just simply to be aware. If you arrive at an airport or a bus station in a few less-developed countries and find yourself surrounded by what may seem like thousands of locals, the main thing to do is not to panic. If you are a bit claustrophobic, you may struggle in the throng of people trying to get your attention. Being a Western backpacker you are seen simply as a Westerner who has money... and compared with the great majority of people that you will meet, you are relatively wealthy. You may be offered everything from taxi rides to watches, from sex to massages.

- Take a deep breath and relax; you are perfectly safe.
- Keep an eye on your belongings, as thieves may take advantage of the crowd and your confusion.

- If there are other backpackers around, stick with them... always a good idea to get talking to other backpackers on the planes/bus who are going to the same destination, remembering that you are all in the same boat. You are then less likely to get ripped off, will feel more secure, and will instantly make some friends.

- If you are by yourself, keep all your money hidden, find out exactly where you want to go, and then find some sort of information place and ask how much you should be paying to get to wherever you want to go. Once you feel confident, go outside and start to haggle a price. This is a talent which will literally grow on you.

- **My favourite technique** is to pull one of the locals confidently to the side, haggle what you think is a decent price, and don't give him the money until you get there and are satisfied that you are actually where you are meant to be.

- Practice always makes perfect, and remember that as a traveller it is your duty to be ripped off every once in a while... it happens to everyone (they're lying if they say otherwise!); just don't get offended if you have lost out on the equivalent of about 10p... forget about it.

    I hope you realise that I am playing on your worst fears here, taking the worst-case scenario that you may have in your head from watching

Beware giving locals the money before you actually get the full service that you have paid for. If they turn round at the end and charge you again, you haven't got a leg to stand on. Half now, and half when we get there seems to do the trick. Try not to get too ripped off!

films/documentaries, and so throwing you in at the deep end as it were. The truth is that it will never be as bad as you may think. The thought of travelling the world can be daunting, especially if you are going to countries where it can be quite difficult. In reality you will invariably be with other backpackers and so find it very easy and safe indeed. However, I'm a great believer that if you expect the worst, everything else from then on in will be easier than expected.

- Never give addresses to locals except in very special circumstances. Everyone will be your friend if there is something that they can get out of it. So be warned. I have been hit by this one. I gave my address to a very polite, educated, good-natured, wealthy Malaysian girl we met on a train, who was after an English pen pal to practise her English with. The first letter was very nice, talking about her life, hobbies, etc. But what I wasn't ready for was the stream of letters that followed from all of her friends asking for marriage, names and addresses of my friends, photos, etc... not very pleasant!

Maps

Don't flap about with them in unfamiliar places too much as they point you out to anyone who cares to notice that you are a tourist and that you're probably lost. If you get lost, ask directions from reputable people who live in houses or work in reputable companies. If they have one leg, sleep rough in the docks, wear an eye patch, and answer to the name of 'Blackbeard', maybe you want to think about asking someone else!

Mechanics

Are you one? Do you know your way around the engine of a car? Well if you've read the part on buying cars (Cars, page 145) then you may well be thinking of a way to earn some money/make friends. When staying in major backpacker places such as Sydney, Cairns, New York, Toronto, etc. make sure that you advertise your services in all the major hostels, as it really is a great way for you to earn a bit of money. If you can confidently assess cars for other backpackers then you will soon find that you are worth your weight in gold on the backpacker circuit. So **GO FOR IT!**

Mopeds/motorbikes/bicycles

Beware when you hire them as there is an age-old scam with disreputable companies following you to your first stopping point, waiting for you to leave the bikes unattended, whipping them, and then charging you for the price of a bike using your passport, which you left with the deposit... as a hostage. Just be aware. Also be very wary of renting them in places like Asia where the roads and the bikes are very badly maintained. Sometimes it can be downright hairy, especially when you find yourself heading downhill doing 60mph on a moped designed to do 30mph tops, with no brakes, but being overtaken by some loony local who's suddenly up for a bit of a race 'weeth thiiis crayzy man from Eeeeengaaaland'! Beware.

Musical instruments

Always great for meeting people/as a talking point. Guitars are the favourites and by the time you come back you will have improved considerably. However, whatever you take, don't take the instrument that you've had for years, as you'd be gutted if you lost it... get a cheap alternative. As for travelling with them – it is possible, just a bit awkward at times. However, I carried my didgeridoo halfway round the world, as well as a surfboard for a while when we were in Australia... it's worth it, so you manage!

Nausea
If brought on by, say, travel sickness can be relieved by ginger (to be taken orally of course!). If you're suffering from sea sickness, try to keep your eyes fixed on a cloud as it tends to balance your eyes and make you feel better.

'No Go areas'
Find out where they are and, well, avoid them... or at least let the gung ho travellers from page 158 go there first and see how they get on before you make your decision. Check out the Foreign Office website: www.fco.gov.uk

Passport
- Ensure now that it is fully up to date and valid for the whole duration of your trip. Trying to renew it with only a few days to go before your plane takes off will only be a major hassle to you, something which you don't need. As for trying to get it renewed when you are thousands of miles from home and moving from country to country... ever tried picking your nose with a pneumatic drill? I think you get the picture... incidentally, what a thought, eh? Many countries won't let you in unless you have a minimum of six months left on your passport. This is a vital bit of kit for your travels – so get it sorted now!
- Check your 'dodgy' stamps as there are some countries that you may find it difficult to get into, such as the Arab and Israeli countries, and anywhere in the West if you are an active member of the PLO.
- Are you dual nationality? If so, do try and get both passports up to date as it may mean more work opportunities for you, and definitely less queuing time at certain countries' borders.
- **Although technically yours, your passport is strictly the property of the British Government.** In the case I outlined above of a few people hiring out mopeds and nicking them back, they usually get away with it by holding your passport as a deposit. Victims are simply 'mugged' of their money, handing it over just to get their passport back. However, your response should be that whenever anyone decides to mess around or play games with you and your passport (effectively holding you to ransom with the use of your passport), get in touch with the Embassy straight away, as they don't tend to see the funny side, and will basically get your passport back for you and probably bring the issue up with the local police. In this case, the mopeds are covered by the insurance anyway. So don't let them mess you around. It is your right to keep hold of your passport and documents at all times.

- In a situation where you think that it may be a bad move to let your passport out of your hands... don't. Just keep hold of it and, in the case of an official/someone else wanting to look through it, allow them to watch as you slowly turn the pages yourself... however, don't do this in a way to antagonise the authorities, as you will only end up wasting your time and maybe get yourself into unnecessary trouble.

Always show the utmost respect for any authority you meet, but always maintain your rights, and never let your documents 'disappear', because you may find that to make them 'reappear' it'll cost you money... so beware.

Patience at borders etc...

Always be patient. You have all the time in the world, so getting angry or being rude will get you absolutely nowhere... in fact, it'll normally get you further away from what you hope to achieve than in the first place. You could therefore be left waiting for hours at border crossings for example. It's funny really, because sometimes as a backpacker you are seen as harmless and so at things like border crossings you are rushed through fairly quickly. However, sometimes this is not the case, and you find yourself being checked, double-checked, searched, etc. The secret is to be as clean and tidy as possible. If you have one of those backpacks where you can zip away all the straps, etc. and carry the bag horizontally like a holdall, all the better. Men, have a shave. Women, if you have long hair, wash it, wear it neatly, and already be dressed in accordance with any rules that the country has... get those legs covered up before you have to be dragged aside and told to do it. I know it can be a bit unfair on you, but at least you're only visiting and don't have to live like that every day, eh?

Photography

- Always take care and be considerate.
- Some people may not like cameras being stuck in their faces, to others it may be considered bad luck as some believe that it takes their spirit away.
- Always ask people's permission and don't push it if they say no, as you'll only end up with your Canon 35mm telephoto lens, great camera, ace photos... bouncing from rock to rock as it finds its own way to the bottom of the canyon!
- Never offer money in exchange for taking a photo. As indicated elsewhere in the book, this may lead to offence, and may also set a precedent for everyone else.

- Politeness, smiles and a bit of cunning will get you all of those unusual photos that you want.
- Try to avoid letting locals take photos of you with your camera. A nice gesture... yes, it usually is. But you may find that one time you will give it to the wrong person who has the speed of Linford Christie, the slipperiness of a snake, and the hiding powers of a golf ball in the Arctic, and who answers to the name of 'Toccohamayeea' ('The Shadow'). Meanwhile at the police station (as you need the report for the insurance)... 'Well, he was an Indonesian male, about 5'5", sandals, black trousers, white shirt, black hair, and also answered to the name of "Made"' (the name given to every first-born male). So with only about 4 million people to choose from... your camera has gone!

Photos

Cameras can be a real pain. If you have a really good one, make sure that it is insured. Unfortunately, having too good a camera may attract the wrong sort of attention, and so may make you unnecessarily on guard too much of the time. If it is too big, you might find it awkward, heavy and bulky. However, if you have a cheap one, the picture quality may not be as good. Not having a zoom lens meant that I have missed out on some great photos... I have been within spitting distance of bears, moose, killer whales, etc., but have no decent photos as with my camera they all seem to be miles away. So unless the thing is actually sitting on my lap, I just don't expect to get a good photo. If I could do it all again I would invest in one of those compact little numbers that has a zoom lens on it. They are now becoming cheaper and cheaper as technology improves and so, if you can afford to, why not invest in one of them? Remember that once you have finished your trip, which will go a lot quicker than expected, the photos will become a big reminder of your time away. One of my biggest regrets is not having a decent camera, as I missed out on some great once-in-a-lifetime photos, as well as many others not coming out.

Digital cameras. I have now just got my first digital camera. It is wicked, takes great shots, loads of them and we simply whack them on the PC and download the wee buggers. Would I take it with me? Probably not, as it is a little expensive and I would need to be able to download images as I went along which could be awkward. However, if you are staying in a place for a while, why not think about taking one if you have one?

Disposable cameras. Have you ever used or thought about using these? I dropped my camera in the sea on the Barrier Reef in Australia, it decided it had had enough of my maltreatment and so decided to give up its fight for life! We were then forced to use disposable cameras. They are actually relatively cheap and the photos that come out really aren't bad at all. I wouldn't recommend them for the whole duration of your trip as it would be cheaper to have a decent camera. However, for certain events during your trip they are a great idea. The waterproof ones are great if you go diving and I've got some wicked shots of me snorkelling on the Barrier Reef. They are also useful and robust enough to take out to beach parties, on any night out, while trekking, and generally on anything that you might do where the camera might get thrown around a bit. On these type of events you can share the cost of buying and developing with a group of friends, allowing you to get some class memorable photos at an affordable price. So if you're all off to some major event that you want to have photos of, arm yourself with one, and split the costs. Ones with a black and white film are worth taking with you as well – as you can get some awesome black and white shots that you can get enlarged and framed at a later date.

Question: Do you develop your photos as you go along?

- If you do, you can write everybody's names, comments, etc. on the back… instead of waiting until you get home, forgetting, and possibly not getting them all down.
- If you don't, it may mean that you literally have hundreds to sort out when you get home, which you may never do… I still haven't done any of mine, and they are now all sitting loose in a box, muddled and in a helluva mess. I think it would take about a week now to get them sorted..
- Getting them developed as you go along will mean that you will spread the cost of development over time, rather than having a massive bill when you finally do get them done.
- However, if you do get them developed, then you have to carry them around with you… they can be heavy, bulky, and may well get damaged.
- But then if you carry your films around with you, you will have to look after them really well to stop them getting wet/damaged! It has also been known for some airport X-ray machines to wipe the films (though most are now film-friendly); you can get special bags to protect the film when passing through an X-ray machine. But, to be sure, get them checked by hand as you go through.

So what do you reckon is the best thing to do? Tony and I actually sent our films home in a package of things from Australia. A good idea, but a risky one, as I'd have been gutted if they had got lost in the post.

Well, each to their own, you just have to do what you think is the best for you.

Plastic bags

Don't stand out as a tourist with a backpack, map, camera and sombrero! By going for a wander around town with your things in a plain white plastic bag, you'll make yourself look ordinary, part of the scene, and so will naturally blend in. Placcy Bs are also great for storing wet things in without making everything else in your bag wet too.

Police

Always go to them if you have any trouble or problems, especially if in Westernised countries. However, be aware that in certain corrupt developing countries you may have to treat them with a little bit of caution. Yes, there are loads of stories that do the rounds about the police in places like Mexico taking your passport from you and then basically 'mugging' you of your money to get it back. I've personally never had any problems, but a couple of my friends have... just be aware of some of the 'tricky things' that they might get up to. Some undercover police have been known to offer drugs to backpackers, arrest them, and then blackmail them of their money so that they don't spend time in a foreign prison. All nasty stuff I'm sure you will agree.

In places like Thailand they really work hard to help backpackers and have set up the Thai Tourist Police. Wanting to get rid of the ugly side of tourism which usually centres around rip-off merchants and con men in bars, clubs and on the beaches, the Tourist Police now have the powers to go into clubs, shops and bars, and quite literally... kick arse! If you have any problems you can go straight to them, as they have the power to close places down. In most places the police are very efficient, so do use them. But if in doubt, get in touch with the Embassy first. Usually 'The tourist is always right', so play on it!

Protection

- The little alarms that you can get over here, you know the ones that I mean, the attack alarms that are issued to women... they are class, and great for your own protection and peace of mind. Having lived in Manchester for three years, I think that women should get used to carrying them around.
- These alarms are nifty little things, small and not very heavy... but, most importantly, they do their job. To an unsuspecting attacker they would give them a serious shock, and so give you the time to get away. They are also great for attracting attention.
- But they are not only for women. You may think that as a bloke you are hard, macho, and beyond being attacked/mugged. I think you've been reading too many comics, lads! It can happen to anyone, so you don't have to feel totally soft if you carry one in your backpack... you never know when it might come in handy.

Dad's Top Tip!

PIN numbers. If you have credit cards and all sorts of other PIN numbers that you need to remember, here's quite a handy way of being able to have them written down and secure at the same time.

On the back of a card of some sort write down in order all the letters of the alphabet from A to Z. Then pick some four letter word that you will remember such as 'BLAG' (a friend of mine Steve's nickname – among others!). Then put your PIN number under those letters in that order, and then fill in all the other letters with other numbers:

My PIN is 8279 (it's not in case you try and nick my card... even I'm not that dumb!!)

A B C D E F G H I J K L M N O P Q R S T U V W X Y Z
7 8 0 3 4 9 9 1 4 6 2 2 4 8 5 1 0 3 3 7 5 8 1 3 8 2

Visa and Access   Steve Freeman

- Some alarms are activated by having a chord pulled out, and are designed so that they can be attached to doors at night... if you feel uneasy, attach it to the door, and if it is opened, the alarm goes off.
- Similarly, you can wander around with the chord round your wrist, and the alarm in your bag. If the bag is snatched, the thief is left with a piercing alarm to get rid of (and so will usually drop the bag and run off).

As for self-protection, I'm a great believer in thinking on your feet, doing the unexpected, and outsmarting any would-be attacker. I have evaded mugging twice, simply by walking straight out in the middle of the road among the traffic, which gave them a bit of a shock, and the second time I pretended to be a 'Manc' (someone from Manchester for those who don't know!) with a fake Manc accent... which put doubt in the bloke's mind about whether I was actually a student ripe for mugging and gave me valuable time to get away. Another great one I have heard is of a woman in an underground car park by herself... she saw a couple of dodgy blokes in between her and her car. She couldn't be sure as to their intentions, so she put her arms up like an aeroplane and then 'flew' to her car making aeroplane noises. They thought she was crazy... and she was safe! There's no point in getting embarrassed about it, you just have to do whatever comes into your head, something unexpected, and then just get out of there. You're never going to see those people again are you?

The Queen

You may be asked many times, 'How is she?' 'She's fine!' as a reply normally does the trick, unless of course you know her personally, where a true account of her well-being might be in order. On no account pretend to be a member of the royal family unless you are an exceptional blagger, or if it may lead to fantastic hospitality and a lot of wealth coming your way. I think it is still classed as treason and will be frowned upon by the government, the royal family, and your host if ever you are found out.

Similarly with Queen the group... in places thousands of miles from home, claiming an association with the band or the late Freddie Mercury, accompanied by a few badly sung versions of their classics, will possibly get you a long way. In fact, this is a great blag to play with any famous personality,

➤ However, do use your judgement to distinguish between adventure and stupidity. Always assess the situation first.

➤ Why not take a quick self-defence class before you go? There are loads of them about at places like local sports centres. Well, why not? You never know when a few techniques might come in handy.

because by the time they find out that Paul McCartney never had a son called Tom, I'll be thousands of miles away anyway!

Rules

All countries have them, whether they are to do with religion, drugs, dress codes, festivals, litter, behaviour or drinking. Make an effort to find out what they are in the countries that you are visiting, and do try and stick to them. Denying knowledge of them will only get you so far, and sometimes nowhere at all (unless you are caught 'jaywalking' like we were in America... to which our response was 'What is "Jaywalking" old chap? Back in England we cross the roads where we like!'... Got us off!).

Shipping/Posting items

Sending things back home can be a great idea. If you find that you have too much stuff, putting a little package together and sending it home is one of the best solutions. If you have been to all the cold countries that you are going to, why not send those heavy jumpers back through the post? The obvious problem is them never reaching the destination. I have seen the best of all the angles... Everything from sending things by air (which can be very expensive, but at least you know that it's got more chance of getting there), to sending it overland. This is the cheaper way, and indeed a package that we sent back from Australia did make it. Looking back, it was quite a dodgy thing to do, as it had all of our films in it to date, and all those bits and pieces that were irreplaceable, such as my bungee-jumping video and photos. However, they got there. But, having nearly killed myself in the heat trying to get a present in the post for my brother Mat's birthday from Fiji, I was gutted to find that it never turned up. It probably never left the island, and may even have ended up back in the shop where I bought it... who knows?

Ship items home sir? Many shops may offer to ship souvenirs back home for you in order to get a sale. Yes, this can work very well, but call me Mr Sceptical as I think of countless items that have got 'lost in the post' and mysteriously never leave the shelf in the shop... It's a long way to go back to ask why they took the money and never posted the damn thing!

Sleeping bags

Make sure that you have the best possible sleeping bag for the climates that you are going to come up against. The sleeping bag that I use is a tiny two-season one that packs away to nothing. In hot countries it is great, as when it is really hot at night I simply lie on it unzipped. The problem is that when it does get fairly cold it is absolutely no use, forcing me to sleep in loads of clothes inside it. The dilemma you'll probably face is how thick a one can you buy and how small will it pack down to. You can buy little compactor bags that you stuff the sleeping bag into and then pull the toggles to compact it down even more, which work very well. With a thicker sleeping bag you do have an advantage in that you are warmer when it gets cold, and when it gets hot you'll simply sleep on top of it anyway. Two- or three-season should be a minimum; three- or four-season if you are going anywhere cold.

- Do think about the weight of it, and how much space it will take up in your pack, as this will start to become quite important as your pack gets fuller and fuller.
- Try to air the sleeping bag as often as you can, as it will tend to sweat and start to smell after a while.
- Remember that you are going to have to get at it virtually every day, so think about this when you are doing your final pack. If your pack has a separate bottom compartment, this is ideal.
- Remember also that in most hostels they require you to have a sleeping sheet, so make sure you get one. The sleeping sheets that are sewn up to give a 'sleeping bag effect' are very useful in that they can give you an extra layer of warmth when it is cold, but you can also fill them with your clothes (and valuables if you want) and use it as a pillow.

Sleeping in airports/bus stations, etc.

Sometimes you may find that this is a good idea if you have a very early bus or plane. It means that you don't have to pay for a night's accommodation that doesn't really get used, and you don't have to get up even earlier to go and catch the flight. The natural worry is going to sleep, waking up, and finding all your belongings gone. If worried, try to sleep 'entangled' in your backpack, or if you have a small chain or cable lock you can secure your pack to the seat. In decent airports you shouldn't have to worry, as there is usually ample security around to watch over you anyway. Beware, it can get very cold even in the hottest of countries, as without the doors constantly opening and closing, the air conditioning works overtime and creates nice Arctic conditions. I experienced this in Brisbane airport and had one of the most uncomfortable nights in my life, wrapped up in about three T-shirts, jeans, towels, etc… not very pleasant!

Tourism Concern

If you are concerned about ethical travel issues and being an ethical traveller, you might want to check these guys out.

Tourism Concern is a UK-based membership organisation which campaigns for ethical and fairly traded tourism, particularly in Third World countries. It forges links with people in destination areas and gives the travelling public, the media and decision-makers in tourist-sending countries information about more ethical travel. Contact:

Tourism Concern
Stapleton House
277–281 Holloway Road
London N7 8HN
Tel: (020) 7753 3330
email: info@tourismconcern.org.uk
website: www.tourismconcern.org.uk

Tourist information booths

Great places, full of information, but hardly ever used! Why not? They'll be able to tell you the cheapest and safest ways to get around, the best deals, etc. They'll also supply you with maps and other useful information such as where to go and, more importantly, where not to go. If they're there, use them. I really don't understand why people have an aversion to them; one of the mysteries of this world!

Touts

In every country they'll always be around to prey on the baffled and bewildered tourists. They will always offer the best deals and often rip you off. Beat them by being confident and prepared. They won't hang around you if you look as though you know what you are doing. Treat dealing with touts and salesmen like a game. By being bold and assertive you can 'play the game'... and win!

Train compartments

Make sure that you lock the door if you are sleeping in a separate one, as tourists are quite vulnerable when on trains. Don't be put off by the stories of the French/Russian bandits chloroforming people in their sleep... yes it did happen in about 1990, but it was very rare. And besides, if it did happen, you wouldn't know about it until you woke up and it was all over. In short, more chance of having an intelligent conversation with a constipated kitten than it happening to you.

Trains/buses/local transport

At each stop keep an eye on your baggage and make sure that it doesn't get off until you decide to (as quite often it will be stored in the compartment under the bus and so could easily be removed without your knowledge... which is another good reason to take off all identifying labels from the outside).

Universities

A constructive gapyear can now help you get into university. As long as you are aware of what you are going to get out of your gapyear and you can get this across to the admissions tutors, then you will really enhance your chances. Whatever you do, DON'T make it sound like you are just going for a holiday. Do, however, show focus, understanding of why you want to take a gapyear and, as mentioned, what you are going to get out of it.

Vegetarians

If you let the airlines know that you are vegetarian when you book the tickets or before you get on the plane, you will normally get the vegetarian meal. The benefits are that they are normally quite good and you will usually be served first. Be aware of your diet, make sure that you get enough protein, etc. day to day. Eating loads of things like bananas, nuts, and fruit for your Vitamin C should keep you nice and healthy. However, due to the general fear among backpackers of dodgy meat in various areas of the world, you'll find that your ranks will swell considerably, especially in India where vegetable curries become the staple diet!

Wildlife

The great myth is that all wildlife will come and attack you. Yet if you think about it, we are a species of 'wildlife' – would you, if you saw a cow walking near you, go and attack it? Would it attack you? Exactly! (There is a kind of logic hidden in there somewhere.) I know there are a lot of exceptions, in that snakes, bears and crocodiles are slightly more dangerous than the odd cow, but the point is that if you make loads of noise then even dangerous animals will move away to avoid a confrontation. If you startle them, some may attack, so by making plenty of noise in forests and areas of long grass, things like snakes

won't sit around and wait to be trodden on. However, if you're travelling during the hibernation season, exceptions have to be made to the noisemaking rule! Being brought up in the UK, the majority of us are totally unused to wildlife, therefore while camping and trekking in areas all over the world it is always a good idea to find out what the locals think about the surrounding wildlife, and digest any tips that they have for you.

Bears for example. Did you know that they can run faster than racehorses, swim faster then Duncan Goodhew and Sharon Davis put together, and can climb trees? Having been brought up on Yogi Bear and Gentle Ben, I was under the impression that I would be able to get away from this big lumbering creature. Guess I was wrong, eh? As for taking one on with a couple of quick Frank Bruno jabs to the head... a fully grown Grizzly can take the head off a moose with just one swipe! Makes you feel pretty vulnerable.

➤ **Wildlife... if you respect it, it will respect you!**

Chapter 13

Coming home

*'The more I see of other countries
the more I love my own'*

Anna Louis de Stael (1807)

Make them proud!

A few final words on the subject of travel

Just to round this little book off. Yes, you will have changed, and for the better I hope. However, don't push this point. I know that I have mentioned it a few times, but it is something that you should notice in yourself, and which others will notice in you. But don't become the 'smart-arse traveller' and start pointing this out to everyone who comes near... you'll do yourself no favours. But I'm sure you're not like that anyway.

You will undoubtedly come across a few problems with friends, even ones that you have had for years. You will find that although you have changed, be it in a big or small way, everyone else is exactly the same as when you left, depending of course on age group, job, college, family commitments, etc. Beware – don't be a travel bore, as it is very easy to slip into. BUT on the other hand, be proud of what you have done and achieved. You must remember that everyone has the chance to do something like this in their life, 99 per cent don't... but you have. Off-the-cuff remarks from many, usually disguised in-jokes aimed at causing you discomfort, is really only jealousy coming out.

Traveller's tales!

You will find that the people who are genuinely interested in where you have been and what you have done will make themselves clear to you. It is with these people that you will be able to share a few of the great things that happened during your trip. A lot of things will happen to you while you are away. Many of them will be amazing things that you will never have even come close to experiencing before. They may have blown your mind, and still give you a great feeling when you think of them. They will also be in the forefront of your mind, and so in general conversation with your mates, while words trigger off thoughts to them of a programme that they saw last week on the television, the same words trigger memories of you white-water rafting in Africa... and you really want to tell them just how much you 'peed your pants'! Unfortunately, most of your mates will be green with envy and will: a) not want to hear it; and b) not understand what you are talking about anyway! This is not your fault, just because you have had a bit of adventure in your life. You will then be barracked by calls of 'traveller's tales again'! I did get this quite a lot at one point. I can take a joke like the rest of them, but it just happened to go on too much, to the point that I got it the whole time and stopped talking about my travels, which is where my best memories are. You must put your foot down, otherwise you may get frustrated and start regretting that you have travelled, something which you must never do. Life is for living. Get on with it and ignore those who are jealous of you or who spout hot air!

It's a narrow-minded world after all!

With new, broadened horizons you will undoubtedly start to find people a bit narrow-minded in a few of their views. I am not being 'yeah well man... I mean... as a traveller man... you have the first-hand knowledge of the world at your fingertips man', as you will have more than gathered now that I'm totally the opposite of that. Do you remember that at the start I made the point of people settling down into their own little worlds that revolve solely around them? This really is true, and it happens in the end to everybody.

The point? Don't travel with your eyes shut. You need to get something from your time away, so make sure you do. Sitting around talking to people from all over the world, seeing different cultures and ways of life, watching, listening, learning... opens your eyes.

More employable?... well, I think so!

I believe that when I left to go travelling for the first time I was a very naïve and cocky 18-year-old, and narrow-minded like the rest. Since coming back, and indeed since travelling some more, I believe that I am a bit more broad-minded about a lot more things. I do believe that I am more employable, and in fact many employers are more than happy to interview people who have had a gapyear and gone travelling, as they are seen as more broad-minded in their views. You will have more to put on your CVs and application forms, and a lot to talk about in your interviews.

A lot of the jobs that I am applying for at the moment have about 3,000 applications for only about 50 places – some have even more!! If you think about how big a pile of 3,000 applications is, you will realise the enormity of the job of selection. You need to make your CV stand out! Add in very brief notes on your things of interest: travelling the world, bungee-jumping, rafting, sailing, funny events that happened. No interest: doing gymnastics at the age of 12, being a member of the school chess club at 14, and winning a Blue Peter badge for a magnificent 'Bring and Buy' sale that you organised in your garage in 1995 which raised £64.72. And remember that everyone 'plays sport' and 'enjoys reading' and 'likes to socialise'. Everyone is also 'highly ambitious' and 'likes to succeed'... but what gives you the qualification to be able to say this?

What they want is evidence that you have a life!

Why are you different from the rest? Why should you be of more interest to them than the next person? Why? Because you have got off your backside and done something that you have wanted to do... and had a ball doing it.

Having undertaken a 'big trip' of some sort you will have exhibited signs of confidence, organisation, planning, decision making, financial control, possibly decisions under pressure, leadership/teamwork skills, etc. Employers now rate initiative, communication skills and decision-making skills above education and social background. They want to see evidence of this on your CV and application form to prove that you are indeed the employable person they have been looking for and who will be an asset to the company.

Margaret Murray, former head of the CBI's Education Policy Group: 'Travel is thought to be a good idea if it gives the young person the "oomph" to start work. But it is not the sort of travel where you wander around the world with a rucksack dreaming. If a young person can answer the question "What has been achieved as a result of the year?" then we would be interested in interviewing them.' Take note!

Itchy feet

When you come back, you may find it difficult fitting back into the old routine for a while, and those itchy feet won't be happy unless they're under a backpack in a strange country thousands of miles from home... 'largeing it up' on a tropical beach, or on the edge of a volcano, in a raging river, or on the steps of one of the wonders of the world! (I'm only saying this to whet your appetite and make you want to go even more!) In fact, I even think to myself, why am I sitting here in this computer room in Suffolk College, type type type type type all day (often wondering what the brunette's name is sitting to the left of me!) when I could be off travelling somewhere? But then I go to the bank and realise why I am still here...! However, for the moment, the memories which accompany me all the time while I'm typing are enough for a simple young pup like myself! But you will fit back into it all; after all, this is your country and your culture... except with tastes of different cultures, you may be a bit more 'cultured' now. Don't bore your friends, don't alienate them, and don't be alienated by them. 'When I was in Australia... ', 'Oh yeah, when I was in Thailand... ' You'll stick out like a punk at a reggae concert, but you will be the last person to realise this. Jealousy can be cruel but will fade away, self-satisfaction and fantastic memories can't be beaten, and will be around forever.

Goodbye and Good Luck

OK, well that's about all from me, I'll take up no more of your time. My aim in this book is to produce something that will be of use to everyone who reads it. Everyone seems to talk about money... will I make any, how much, etc., etc. The truth is that I really don't know, and to be honest I really don't care. I wrote this book when I was 22 years old; I had no job and was financing myself by digging into my student loans and busking with my didgeridoos. Yeah, financially I could be doing better, but the thing is that I am ecstatically happy with my life... how many people can say that? A few years on and I've updated this third edition – but I'm still travelling, still passionate about gapyear travel (I now run the gapyear.com website)... and I'm still ecstatically happy with my life!

I have had my struggles, like everyone else, and when I wrote this book the struggle with my Dad was still going on. In a way this book is really dedicated to him, as I hope that he realises that I am an adult now, and that I am in control of my own life. At present, I am achieving goals and ambitions. I love it! I hope that one day he will be able to turn round and tell me that, yes, he is proud of me. But until that day, my life goes on.

I will always strive to get the most out of my life, and enjoy it as only I know how... by living every day and every opportunity to the full. I strive to be 'larger than life', and my hope is that you will too. I want this book to be of use to every potential young backpacker out there. The world is out there. Why not live your dreams? What is stopping you?... well Jack really! So do it, go for it, and have a great time. The fact that you are at this point in the book means that you are about to go anyway, so I'll hold you up no longer. All I say is Good Luck, and do send me a postcard (via the Publisher please, address on page iv) or email if you like – tom@gapyear.com, as I'd love to hear how you are getting on.

Have fun, travel safely and keep in touch.

Things to do
check list

OK, a little organisation doesn't do anyone any harm, and in fact you may find that it does in fact do you a bit of good. There are a lot of things that you have to remember, other things that you may not realise have to be done... and if you have a memory like mine, you're going to need to note a few things down somewhere. Normally I get a little notebook to note times, appointments, meetings, etc., down. This is much better than the old system of writing these things on pieces of paper and having them loose on the desk in my room. As a result, in the past I have forgotten about doctor's appointments, picking up travellers' cheques and a few other mundane things that have to be done.

So I thought about what would be of use to you, and have laid the following out in a way which I hope you will find useful enough to use. Anything related to the preparation for your trip can be noted down in the next few pages, so you can keep everything together and find it all at a glance. It really is worth doing you know, so give it a go. I've tried to put some sort of order into the list, so you don't find that you've got a couple of days until take-off, and absolutely shedloads left to do. Plan early, and everything will run smoothly.

To make life a little easier for you, there is a 'One-stop-shop' section on gapyear.com in the 'Travel' zone where we have identified the top five to ten organisations in each area for you to save you time and money when you are shopping around. Other travellers have also come into this area and added reviews of their own to help you make your choices. The website is well worth a visit when you are at the serious preparation stage, or even just to find out what is available to help you get your ass in gear!

Getting your flight

When you have some time free, call in to a travel agent's and pick up all the brochures that you think might be applicable. Dream for a while about what you think you might like to do, and where you might like to go. The brochures are class, as they are full of all those glossy pictures that you really want to see. This is the very first step, which will get you in the mood. Take them home and spend a weekend, or a couple of days, flicking through them, looking at the pictures, and seeing the places you would like to visit.

Read 'Guide to buying a flight' on gapyear.com.

Set a day to visit/call a student travel agent to get a quote. Remember to have in your mind a rough itinerary of where you would like to go and when, so they can plug your dates and destinations into the computer to give you a quote. There is nothing they can do for you if you just turn up and say 'I would like to go around the world please!' However, while you are there chat through a few alternatives, ask them to suggest some other destinations and see if there are any special offers available: e.g. Air New Zealand has been known to allow unlimited free stop-overs in as many Pacific islands as you like.

Recommended travel agents/flight companies

STA Travel
Tel: (020) 7361 6129
www.statravel.co.uk

STA Travel is the largest student/youth travel agent in the UK with over 50 branches in the UK and over 300 worldwide. It specialises in fares for students and those under 26. It has been around for a long time and so is a very good, solid, international company. My advice would be that you should definitely get a quote from STA Travel to give you something to measure against and, as the biggest, it can often get specials the others can't. Great monthly emailed newsletter, by the way.

www.roundtheworldflights.com
Tel: 0870 442 4842

As the name suggests, these guys are a specialist round-the-world flight company. Set up a few years back by a really cool guy called Nick Pulley, this is now part of a bigger set-up called Global Village. Nick is still in charge of this area and as a result the customer service is pretty good. Staff are young, knowledgeable and enthusiastic whenever I have called. The site enables you to create your own itineraries. Worth getting a quote if you are thinking about buying a round-the-world ticket and also to help you think about where you want to go.

Austravel
Tel: 0870 166 2020
www.austravel.com

I would always recommend Austravel for a quote, especially if you are thinking about going to Australia. You never know what they might have.

Over 26? Yup, there are some specialist companies out there for you wrinklies, too, close to bus routes as well so the bus pass will come in handy! If you are over 26 the two companies below, in my view, are the best place to start for quotes (you can also use roundtheworldflights.com as above as they have no age limit).

Bridge the World

Tel: 0870 443 2399
www.bridgetheworld.com

Set up a long time ago by a bloke called Mr Bridge (kinda like this story behind the name!). Anyone I have ever spoken to who has used them has always quoted amazing customer service, competitive prices, etc. So I guess this speaks for itself.

Trailfinders

Tel: (020) 7628 7628
www.trailfinders.com

Very similar to Bridge the World but they have more branches around the country (thirteen to Bridge the World's three). The couple of times I have been in the service has been good, prices competitive, etc. – everything you need really.

Quick note about online flight companies

There are loads of them – cheapthis.com, bargainthat.com, the most amazingsomethingelse.co.uk. Most of them use the same fare engines and so you will just be booking from them – they just use the domain name to get people through the door. If you are doing a trip that is longer than your two-week piss-up in Benidorm, then you need to think about customer service, the ability to change tickets, sort out problems, etc. Be wary of websites that look cheap and feel like they have been around for a few minutes, i.e. they may disappear when you are mid-trip! Look for history, a good, solid, preferably big, company behind the website/domain name.

OK... enough of the tips, let's crack on!

Flight quote assistant

Need help?

There is a 'Guide to buying a round-the-world flight' on gapyear.com and a list of companies to save you piling through the thousands of options you'll get from the search engines.

Travel agent:
Tel./website:
Date and time called:
Spoke to:
Quote:
Notes:

Travel agent:
Tel./website:
Date and time called:
Spoke to:
Quote:
Notes:

Travel agent:
Tel./website:
Date and time called:
Spoke to:
Quote:
Notes:

Visas

There are visa companies around that you can pay to help you get a visa: e.g. for Australia quite a well-known company is Visas Australia (Tel: (01270) 626626, www.visas-australia.com). Companies like these take the hassle out of it all.

Make a list of countries you need visas for.

Country	Visa available before you go?	Notes

Insurance

This is something that, if you have read this book through, you'll know I am really passionate about. For the last time – **YOU NEED TO TAKE OUT INSURANCE!!** Why? If you don't something may happen which could land you with a bill for more than £500,000 (the largest claim I heard of was for £1.2 million). Don't ever be in the position where your family have lost their homes and everyone is bankrupt because you couldn't be arsed to get insurance or because you thought it was smart to save a few quid!

Need help?

There is a 'Guide to buying insurance' on gapyear.com and a list of companies to save you trawling through the thousands of options you'll get from the search engines. Beware of online companies who haven't been around for long and whose insurance looks too cheap – it is for a reason! Go for credibility. A good place to start is www.noworriesinsurance.com, something I have been involved in putting together with a reputable insurance company.

Insurance company:
Tel./website:
Date and time called:
Spoke to:
Quote:
Notes:

Insurance company:
Tel./website:
Date and time called:
Spoke to:
Quote:
Notes:

Insurance company:
Tel./website:
Date and time called:
Spoke to:
Quote:
Notes:

Medical/Health

Arrange a doctor's appointment asap. It is important that you have a check-up before you go.

Don't forget to discuss:
- regular medicine you may take
- malaria if you are going to an 'at-risk area'
- the Pill, and other contraception queries (free condoms are available at Family Planning)
- allergies
- travel sickness (if you suffer from it)
- any other questions. Don't be shy... if you have a medical question it's better to ask now than to regret not asking about it
- getting a note about any medication that you take regularly and that you may have to take with you. There are different brand names for drugs in different countries, so it is important to take information on what exactly goes into the medication so if you need to replace it overseas they can find you the equivalent drug
- your appendix. Is it still in? If it is, ask:
  - where is it located
  - what pains are associated with appendicitis
  - how to diagnose that you have it
  - what to do if you have it.

Action	Date	Notes
Arrange doctor's appointment		
Injections (e.g. which ones, dates, notes, etc.)		
Starting a course of tablets? (e.g. malaria)		
Prescriptions		
Contraception		

Work checklist

Here's a list of things to sort out at work before you leave:

Action	Date	Notes
Hand notice in		
Get references		
Create CV and email it to yourself		
Tax rebate due		
Apply for jobs		

Finances

If you haven't already done it, it is important to get a budget sorted out for your trip sooner rather than later. There isn't enough room here to do it so, if you are computer literate, get onto Excel or something and set up a spreadsheet to work out all the following:

- money you will leave with (money you are earning minus all taxes, what you will spend on tickets, etc.)
- a rough budget for your WHOLE trip (includes food, accommodation, transport, socialising, etc., daily, weekly and monthly – use the Rough Guide, Lonely Planet and Footprint guidebooks to help you here). Also plan for tours, activities and events (will you bungee-jump, raft, take a tour to the Barrier Reef, scuba dive, see a Madonna concert?).

Need help?

Gapyear.com has a 'Guide to creating a travel budget' and also a 'Guide to fundraising' which may be of use. In the 'Travel' zone there is also a list of all the companies you may well end up using, so you can get an idea about how much stuff costs to help you budget and read the reviews of others to see whether things are worth doing or not.

Your budget summary

	Value/cost	Notes
Daily travel budget		
Weekly travel budget		
Monthly travel budget		
Extras to budget for (e.g. bungee-jump, tours. etc.)		
Additional transport costs		
Cost of travel kit (e.g. backpack, sleeping bag, etc.)		
How much will you leave with?		
Total budget (brace yourself!)		

Finances checklist

Action	Date	Notes
Meeting with the bank?		
Travellers' cheques: order/ pick up		
Foreign currency: order/ pick up		
International debit card: got one/need a new one?		
Credit card: sort out all issues		
Power of attorney: give to parents/family/friend		

General and emergency photocopying checklist

Check that all your documents are up to date with all the correct contact details, personal details, valid dates, etc. Also remember that it is important to photocopy everything and leave copies with friends and family. I suggest you do four copies – one for your parents, one for a trusted mate, one for another family member (in case your parents are away), and a set to take with you. Should things go wrong you will have proof of the existence of 'things', which should help solve problems and get new 'things' issued. I would also advise emailing all important stuff to yourself.

VERY IMPORTANT NOTE

1. Taking photocopies of things like your credit cards that can be easily stolen is NOT a good idea.

2. Emailing all your personal details to your email account is something I do BUT I have to remind you that this is NOT completely secure.

3. Make sure the people who have the copies know why they have them, i.e. to help you out when you need it. I would suggest creating a plan – which includes knowing how to get hold of these important people (take mobile numbers, email addresses, a note of holidays, etc.).

What is it?	Up to date/ sorted	Photo-copied?	Emailed to you/ others?	Notes
Passport (+ number, date issued, etc.)				
Insurance certificate + emergency contact details				
Travellers' cheques: serial numbers				
Flight tickets + contact details				
References				
CV				
Medical documents				
Medical 'stuff'				

What is it?	Up to date/ sorted	Photo-copied?	Emailed to you/ others?	Notes
Evidence of injections				
Credit cards + emergency numbers				
International debit card + emergency numbers				
Evidence of qualifications				
Visas				
Embassy addresses/ details				
All emergency contact details				
Itinerary				
Pre-paid tour/ activity details + contact details				
Driving licence				
International driving licence				
Glasses/contact lens prescription				
Serial numbers for valuables, e.g. camera				
Memberships, e.g. International Youth Hostels, ISIC				
AA/car breakdown club				
Other				

Clothes/travel kit

Clothes and travel kit are very particular things to everyone. Things to think about are:

- making use of birthdays and Christmas to save you money
- consider buying certain items overseas where they might be cheaper, e.g. clothes in most developing nations or the USA
- borrowing things
- not taking things you don't need or will hardly use.

Birthday/ Christmas pressies	Stuff you need to buy	What can you borrow?	Things you really need

ONE MONTH TO GO

Note down all the things you need to do in your last month and get them done!

ONE WEEK TO GO!

If this section isn't actually big enough to use you may want to print out something bigger and stick it on your wall. Last-minute things are always the hardest to get done in the short space of time and easiest to forget. SO WRITE EVERYTHING DOWN and get help from others if you are starting to get behind.

7 DAYS TO GO   ___/___/___

6 DAYS TO GO   ___/___/___

5 DAYS TO GO   ___/___/___

4 DAYS TO GO   ___/___/___

3 DAYS TO GO   ___/___/___

2 DAYS TO GO   ___/___/___

1 DAY TO GO   ___/___/___

D–DAY... YOU'RE OFF, HAVE A GREAT TIME!

PACKING CHECKLIST

Essentials

- ❑ Passport
- ❑ Visas
- ❑ Immunisation record
- ❑ All tickets
- ❑ Insurance
- ❑ Travellers' cheques
- ❑ All emergency numbers
- ❑ Sleeping bag
- ❑ Sleeping sheet
- ❑ Mosquito net
- ❑ Peg-free washing line
- ❑ Guidebooks
- ❑ Diary
- ❑ Pens

- ❑ Glasses/contact lenses
- ❑ Photocopies of documents
- ❑ Moneybelt
- ❑ Poncho
- ❑ Medi and sterikit
- ❑ Sunglasses
- ❑ Camera
- ❑ Film
- ❑ Student identity cards
- ❑ ISIC card
- ❑ Passport photos (min. of 6)
- ❑ Sewing kit
- ❑ Spare eyeglasses
- ❑ Prescriptions

Hardware

- ❑ Watch
- ❑ Travel alarm
- ❑ Flashlight
- ❑ Candles
- ❑ Swiss army knife
- ❑ Universal sink plug
- ❑ Adapter plugs

- ❑ Combination padlocks
- ❑ Chain – link, bike or wire
- ❑ Spare batteries
- ❑ Whistle
- ❑ Personal alarm
- ❑ Walkman or CD player
- ❑ Camera

Toiletries

- ❑ Ear plugs
- ❑ Tissues (big box)
- ❑ Shampoo
- ❑ Conditioner
- ❑ Safety pins
- ❑ Tampons
- ❑ Sanitary towels
- ❑ Condoms
- ❑ Contraception
- ❑ Sun cream
- ❑ Lip balm
- ❑ Insect repellent

- ❑ Flannel
- ❑ Brush or comb
- ❑ Deodorant
- ❑ Toothbrush and paste
- ❑ Shaving stuff
- ❑ Toilet paper
- ❑ Wet wipes
- ❑ Dental floss
- ❑ Moisturiser
- ❑ Medication
- ❑ Nail clippers
- ❑ Travel wash

Clothes

- ❏ Underwear
- ❏ Shorts
- ❏ T-shirts
- ❏ Cotton shirts
- ❏ Jeans
- ❏ Shoes
- ❏ Sarong
- ❏ Skirt
- ❏ 'Beach pants'
- ❏ Belt
- ❏ Swimming 'things'
- ❏ Long-sleeved shirts
- ❏ Long-sleeved T-shirts
- ❏ Sweater
- ❏ Sun hat/cap
- ❏ Woolly hat
- ❏ Light waterproof top

Scarf and gloves if you are going anywhere cold
Thermal underwear – long-johns are great when it gets cold

Smart clothes

- ❏ Trousers
- ❏ Shirt
- ❏ Skirt
- ❏ Little black number
- ❏ Tie
- ❏ Bow tie
- ❏ Smart shoes
- ❏ Smart sandals

Medical bits and pieces

- ❏ Medi kit
- ❏ Steri kit
- ❏ Adhesive bandages
- ❏ Anti-diarrhoea medicine
- ❏ Motion sickness medication
- ❏ Vitamins
- ❏ Medic Alert identification
- ❏ Water purification tablets
- ❏ Thermometer
- ❏ Antibiotic cream
- ❏ Anti-fungal foot powder
- ❏ Throat lozenges
- ❏ Sharp-ended tweezers
- ❏ Pointed scissors

Paperwork

- ❏ Books
- ❏ Phrasebook
- ❏ Address book
- ❏ Telephone card
- ❏ Job reference letter
- ❏ Family/homelife photos

Other useful items

- ❏ Re-sealable bags
- ❏ Large black bin bag
- ❏ A ball of string
- ❏ Knife/fork/spoon set
- ❏ Eye shade
- ❏ Compass
- ❏ Head torch
- ❏ Inflatable neck pillow

FINAL PREPARATION CHECKLIST

- ❏ Trial packing
- ❏ Penultimate pack
- ❏ Final packing
- ❏ Got all tickets
- ❏ Picked up money
- ❏ Picked up travellers' cheques
- ❏ Sorted all banking/finance issues
- ❏ Organised lift to the airport/station
- ❏ Got everyone's contact details/emails
- ❏ Told everyone who needs to know that you are off and emailed your itinerary and how/when you want them to contact you
- ❏ Sorted all issues with girlfriend/boyfriend/partner
- ❏ Done all photocopies
- ❏ Given photocopies to others
- ❏ Emailed everything to yourself/others

- ❏ Picked up medication/health stuff
- ❏ Ensure travel partner ready
- ❏ Sorted final stuff with family/friends
- ❏ Organised first-night accommodation
- ❏ Know roughly what you are doing for the first three days?
- ❏ Sorted snacks/drinks for the plane/airport in case of delays
- ❏ Organised farewell party (NB: Only do one and do it just before you leave – if people ask 'Haven't you gone yet?' either (a) you have got the timing wrong or (b) you are milking it!)
- ❏ Currently cursing me for making it all sound so easy?

NOTES

Appendix 2

Good books on the market

Travelling accounts

Read how others have tackled an adventure. Great fun, great inspiration! I've added two books from a good mate of mine, Richard Knight, who, despite being a bit of a monkey, has produced a two crackers.

Benedict Allen et al *More Great Railway Journeys*
Ffyona Campbell *Feet of Clay* – her epic walk across Australia
Ffyona Campbell *On Foot Through Africa*
Ffyona Campbell *The Whole Story*
Nick Danziger *Danziger's Adventures*
Nick Danziger *Danziger's Travels*
Josie Dew *Travels in a Strange State – Cycling across the USA*
Kuki Gallmann *I Dreamed of Africa*
Howard Jacobson *In the Land of Oz*
Richard Knight *The Blues Highway*
Richard Knight *Trekking in the Moroccan Atlas*
Irma Kutz *The Great American Bus Ride*
Matthew Parris *Inca – Kola: A traveller's tale of Peru*
Vicki Couchman *A Trail of Visions*
Mark Tully *The Heart of India*
Ronald Wright *Time Among the Maya – Travels in Belize, Guatamala, and Mexico*

Gapyear guides

Val Butcher *Taking a Year Off*
Susan Griffith *Taking a Gapyear* (great book but no relation!)
Susan Griffith *Work Your Way Around The World*
Mark Hempshell *Planning your Gapyear*
Suzannah Hecht *The Gapyear Guidebook*

Novels

Maria Coffey *Three Moons in Vietnam*
Michael Crichton *Travels*
Jack Kerouac *On the Road*

Jane Robinson *Unsuitable for Ladies – An Anthology of Women Travellers*
Jon Swain *River of Time*
Paul Theroux *The Pillars of Hercules* (plus many more books if you like this author)

Humorous travelling accounts
Bill Bryson *Made in America*
Bill Bryson *Neither Here Nor There*
Bill Bryson *Notes From a Small Island*
Bill Bryson *The Lost Continent*
Billy Connolly *World Tour of Australia*
Joseph O'Connor *The Irish Male – at home and abroad*
P.J. O'Rourke *Holidays in Hell*
Michael Palin *Around the World in 80 Days*
Michael Palin *Pole to Pole*

Informative travel
John Hatt *The Tropical Traveller*
Mark Hodson *Your Passport to Safer Travel*
May Morris *Nothing to Declare: Memoirs of a Woman Travelling Alone*
Rough Guides *Women Travel*
Rough Guides *Special More Women Travel*

Travel guides
There are a number of travel guides around. They are all similar in content but completely different in style. My suggestion would be that you look at them all and work out which is the best style for you.

Footprint	slightly fewer titles than the others but a nice new style and becoming increasingly popular
Lonely Planet	the original guidebook covering virtually everywhere on the planet
Rough Guides	second in size to Lonely Planet but with a fresher style and a superb additional range of guides on world music, the Internet, etc.
Trailblazer	small specialist guides

Appendix 3

Useful addresses, telephone numbers and websites

Advice and information websites

www.1000traveltips.org

Want to know which is Vietnam's best Sunday market or where to eat on a budget in Damascus? Try this – a no-frills, but hugely interesting list of tips and suggestions.

www.africaguide.com

Great gapyear advice. An excellent guide to the 51 countries in Africa, covering medical and travel advice, together with links to local attractions, businesses and sites.

www.aussiebackpacker.com.au

A site dedicated to budget travel in, guess where? Australia, with up-to-date information about accomodation, entertainment, transport and other tips.

www.backpackeressentials.com.au

A budget traveller's guide to backpacking the world, this is the Internet version of an Australian magazine. You'll find out the latest news about hostels, features on locations and book reviews.

www.gapyear.com

The place to head to once you put this book down!

www.globetrotters.co.uk

A forum for adventurers, where you can exchange information and advice on travelling.

www.goabroad.com

This US site is great for all gappers and student travellers. Here, you'll find information on unusal destinations.

www.journeywoman.com

Girl-friendly cities, travelling tips and travel tales. There's also advice on what it is and isn't appropriate to wear in different countries, plus tips on travelling safely.

www.lonelyplanet.com

Guidebooks to almost every destination; best for experienced travellers eager to get as much as possible from their trip.

www.mapsworldwide.co.uk

Check out your destination. Also worth trying is multimap.com.

www.roughguides.com

Great guides to countries and cities, plus a reader forum and stacks of links and tips on locations.

www.timeout.com

Want to go clubbing in Cuba or shopping in Singapore? Find out where all the best gigs, festivals and exhibitions are before you go.

www.travel-library.com

A personal guide to travelling round the world compiled by someone who's done it.

www.travel.state.gov

Advice from the US Department of State, which includes lists of current danger zones to avoid.

www.vtourist.com

Concise guides to local transport and visitor information for an impressive range of cities and countries.

www.worldtimeserver.com

World Time Server provides the most accurate local times of any world clock on the Internet.

British Government advice numbers

Foreign and Commonwealth office
(020) 7270 1500 – a 24-hr, first contact number
(020) 7008 0232/0233 – travel advice unit
www.fco.gov.uk and
www.fco.gov.uk/knowbeforeyougo

Health advice for travellers
0800 555777
HM Customs and Excise advice centre
(020) 7928 3344

Home Office – drug/medication questions
(020) 7273 3806
London School of Tropical Medicine
(020) 7636 8636
NHS Direct
0845 4647
www.nhsdirect.nhs.uk
Passport enquiries
08705 210410
www.ukpa.gov.uk
www.knowhow.co.uk
Tourism Concern
(020) 7753 3330
info@tourismconcern.org.uk
www.tourismconcern.org.uk

Email and cybercafés

Cybercafes.com

Visit before you go to find your local cybercafé – you'll be able to keep in touch with friends and family cheaply and quickly by emailing them while you're away. This website contains a list of over 4,000 Internet cafés around the globe.

Set up a free email account with:

www.compuserve.com
www.hotmail.com
www.Lycos.com
www.yahoo.com

Finances

**www.mastercard.com/
cardholderservices/atm**

With more than 601,000 holes-in-the-wall, you can use your Mastercard to get cash almost anywhere in the world.

www.visa.com/pd/atm

This site lists all the cashpoint machines where your Visa card can get you money, as well as offering advice on what to do if you lose it.

www.x-rates.com

The easiest online currency converter to use. Let the handy calculator do all the sums for you.

Health
www.cdc.gov/travel

This US government site from the National Center for Disease Control gives up-to-date information on the latest disease outbreaks around the world, plus essential advice on vaccinations and how to avoid illness while abroad.

www.tmvc.com.au/info10.html

For the paranoid hypercondriac; find out about deep vein thrombosis, intestinal infections and the top 10 diseases of the day. Helpfully, it lists which vaccinations you'll need.

www.tripprep.com

Another useful site to check out, with facts about dozens of ailments, including treatment guidelines and coping with an emergency.

www.who.int/ctd

The World Health Organizations's website provides a fact sheet on all the world's major diseases.

Hostels and accommodation
www.sleepingairports.net

It's free, so why not consider sleeping in an airport? Here's a list of the best and worst.

www.iyhf.org

Home of the International Youth Hostel Federation, you can find out all about your chosen hostel, check availability and even book-in.

www.hostels.com

An independent viewpoint of hostels worldwide.

Travel agencies
STA Travel
(020) 7361 6262 worldwide

www.statravel.co.uk

One of the most popular shops, offering tailor-made deals for student and young, independent travellers.

Trailfinders
www.trailfinders.co.uk

The largest UK independent travel company, with good itineraries and access to discount flights.

Flight Centre and Student Flights
Tel: 08708 900092
www.studentflight.co.uk

Flight Centre is one of the world's largest independent travel agents. Student Flights is its youth travel brand.

Roundtheworldflights.com
Tel: 0870 442 4842
www.roundtheworldflights.com

A great site which enables you to tailor-make your own round-the-world trip.

www.austravel.com

Part of Thomson Travel, this company specialises in flights and accommodation for young travellers.

www.travelcuts.com
A French travel firm with good deals for travellers.

Cheap flights

Most online travel agents offer cut-price tickets, or check out the airline websites – they often have deals advertised via email or just on their site.

www.airtickets.co.uk
www.cheapflights.co.uk
www.deckchair.com
www.dreamticket.com
www.ebookers.com
www.expedia.co.uk
www.flightline.co.uk
www.flightsavers.co.uk
www.lastminute.com
www.majortravel.co.uk
www.orbitz.com
www.stratfordtravel.co.uk
www.trailfinders.com
www.travelocity.co.uk
www.uk-bargains.co.uk

Ferry operators and ports

Brittany Ferries
08705 360360
www.brittanyferries.com
Portsmouth–St Malo, Caen
Poole–Cherbourg
Plymouth–Roscoff

Hoverspeed
08705 240241
www.hoverspeed.co.uk
Dover–Calais, Ostend
Newhaven–Dieppe (Sea Cat and ferries)

P&O Stena Line
08705 980980
www.posl.com
Dover–Calais, Zeebrugge

Stena Line
08705 707070
www.stenaline.co.uk
Fishguard–Rosslare
Holyhead–Dun Laoghaire, Dublin
Harwich–Hook of Holland
Stranraer–Belfast

Train and tunnel
Eurotunnel
08705 353535
www.eurotunnel.com
Shuttle for cars and coaches only between Folkestone and Calais.

Eurostar
08702 649899
www.eurostar.com

Travelling around

Bus
www.buslines.com.au
A directory for all bus and coach travel in Australia.

www.greyhound.com
America's most famous company offers a great way to cross the States. Book here.

www.ticabus.com
The Tica bus company can take you across Central America. You can't book online, but you can use the timetable to plan your trip.

Train

www.budgettravel.com

A destination and travel information site with dozens of links to sites with detailed train information in specific countries.

www.eurorailways.com

Advice on the best type of pass to buy, as well as timetables and journey planning. You can book online too. See also www.eurostar.com

www.geocities.com/capitolhill/ 5355/

A useful listing of all known websites with information on public transport in North and South America.

www.gsr.com.au

Find out more about Australia's great train journeys, such as Sydney to Perth or Melbourne to Adelaide. You can't book online.

www.railserve.com

In part, a site for anoraks who like trains, but also a darn good timetable guide for trains in Africa, Australia, Europe and North and South America.

www.trainweb.org.indiarail

India has Asia's largest rail network, covering 62,000km. Use this unofficial guide to find out more about it, plus some train times. For more information look up www.indianrailway.com, the offical guide to India's railways.

Can't afford to travel?

There are plenty of organisations that are waiting to help you fund your travel with a grant or sponsorship. Try these:

Lions Club International
(01245) 325752

London Chamber of Commerce
(020) 7248 4444

Rotary International
(020) 7487 5429

Round Table
(0121) 456 4402

Working abroad

Want to work abroad? You'll probably need a visa.
Australia – www.australia.org.uk
USA – www.usembassy.org.uk

www.travelnotes.org

General advice on working abroad, with hints and tips on what you can (and cannot) do in a specific country.

www.allabroad.com

This is one of the largest and most useful sources of information on studying and working abroad. Use the database to find the most up-to-date advice on different work progammes abroad.

Acknowledgements

I would like to thank a whole group of people without whom I would not have been able to attempt this book:

Brothers **Mat** and **Rob**, the Bruton sisters – **Alison** and **Katie**, **Claire Eely-Sedding** (and of course Mrs D!), **Helena Sampson, Jane Stuart, Colin Pidgeon, Jason Race** and **John Taylor** for help with the computer problems, **Tim Jones** for inspiration, **Rob LeMare, SJA Canavan, Jerry Tate, Martin 'Props' Holland, little Cathy Cobley, Lyndsey Underhill, Philippa Symonds, Dawn Howell, Ed** and **Penny, Kirsten Whiting, Steve Butterworth** for his timely advice, **Dom Etheridge** for his motivation and support, **Nina** and **Tania** – my Canadian Girlies, **Ed** and **Jo** for their kindness and so subsequent inspiration (and forgiveness for my 'blunder' at their wedding – bit of a classic though!), **Ben Slater** my diabetic literary master, **Penny Bell** for her guidance, **Alan Bettles** for accompanying me during those long hours at the computer, and of course **Suffolk College** (and **Gillian** at reception) for the use of their computers and allowing me to finish this book off; and my proof readers: **Richard 'oofy' Mortimer** for a fantastic job way beyond the call of duty, **Chris Welburn, Steve Freeman, Danielle O'Malley, Amanda Harris, Dan Woods, Simon Marsh, Stephanie Jones** and **Oliver Baxter** (the last three of whom have taken the book quite literally, and who at the time of publication are off travelling the world... see, it does work!); cartoonist **Dave Upson** – I'm sure you'll agree with me that this lad has a great talent, and I am very thankful for his enthusiasm and co-operation, and his determination to step forward and take up the challenge.

Special mentions also to **Suzie Money** – a remarkable woman who gave me the invaluable confidence I needed; **Marcus Orlovsky** and **Nena Dowse** – unknown to them, they have been major influences on my thoughts and way of life – many thanks; **Jeremy Greenwood**, the original publisher, for taking the punt with me; **Simon Collin** and the guys at Aspect Guides for taking my baby over from Jeremy, and for selling out to the Harry Potter marvels at Bloomsbury. Bloomsbury, my thanks to Faye Carney, Nicola Reisner, Kathy Rooney, Nicky Thompson and Gordon Kerr for the new edition. Five years, one book, three publishers – bring it on! **Jez** – the South African IT legend, for his unrelenting hard work.

Subject index

Gapyear
planning
made
easy
Learn more about
saving for your gapyear
at www.gapyear.com
Published by Barclays Bank PLC. Buisness Banking Marketing Services.
Reg. No 1026167. Registered in England. Reg. Office: 54 Lombard Street,
London EC3P 3AH. A00795
BARCLAYS
FLUENT IN FINANCE